GRUMPY OLD MEN
ON HOLIDAY

GRUMPY

A Manual for th

DAVID QUANTICK

OLD MEN
ON HOLIDAY

British Malcontent abroad

HarperCollins*Publishers*

HarperCollins*Entertainment*
An imprint of HarperCollins*Publishers*
77–85 Fulham Palace Road,
Hammersmith, London W6 8JB

www.harpercollins.co.uk

Published by HarperCollins*Entertainment* 2005

1

A catalogue record for this book
is available from the British Library

ISBN 0 00 720185 0

Set in Adobe Garamond

Printed and bound in Great Britain by
Clays Limited, St Ives PLC

ACKNOWLEDGEMENTS

ONCE AGAIN, WITH THE UNVARYING REPETITIVENESS OF A WASTED LIFE, I MUST THANK KATE HALDANE FOR HER AGENTING SKILLS AND JON NAISMITH FOR HIS EXCELLENT EDITING. I COULD NOT HAVE DONE IT WITHOUT THEM.

To my Mum and Dad, Sheila and Mike,

who never took us on an unmemorable holiday.

CONTENTS

∽

INTRODUCTION 9

PLANNING THE THING 13

Pre-holiday gloom • travel shows • brochures • brochures 2 • travel brochure jargon • online booking • holiday checklists • online booking 2 • holiday insurance • jabs and pills • travel agents

WHAT HOLIDAY? 27

Family holidays • honeymoons • inter-railing • student exchange holidays • backpacking 1 • backpacking 2 • backpacking 3 • hitch-hiking • walking holidays • cycling holidays • activity holidays • climbing holidays • Saga holidays • beach resort holidays • sailing holidays • cruises • Disney • canal holidays • camping holidays • skiing holidays • surfing holidays • caravan holidays • eco holidays • Christmas breaks • package holidays • 18–30 holidays • holidays that end up on cable TV • space holidays • 'dangerous holidays' • holidays in places where books and films have been set • holiday camps • redcoats and bluecoats • murder mystery weekends • holiday cottages 1 • holiday cottages 2 • heritage properties • Las Vegas locations • a London weekend • the 10 most popular holiday destinations

GETTING THERE 85

Packing • leaving the house 1: the papers and the milk • leaving the house 2: giving the keys to the neighbours • leaving the house 3: timers • passport 1 • passport 2 • leaving the house 4 • leaving the house 5 • kennels • plants • driving to the airport/ferry port/railway station • coaches • ferries • airport terminals • airport parking • airport staff • airport shops • bureau de change • luggage trolleys • stupid security questions • gates • moving walkways • the blue electric cart thing • upgrades • classes • airline passengers • short flights • long flights • really long flights • baggage carousel • duty free

THEM AND US 112

Them: the Germans • the French • the Spanish • the Italians • the Dutch • the Belgians • Scandinavians • the Russians • the Japanese • Australians • New Zealanders • South Africans • Canadians • Americans

Us: Britain • Ireland • the Welsh • the Scots • the Cornish • the English • the North • the South • the Isle of Wight • the Isle of Man • the Channel Islands • London • ex-pats

NOW WHAT? 155

The world's most popular tourist attractions • hotels • how not to write a postcard • bumbags • holiday snaps • holiday friendships • holiday romances • swimming costumes • the hotel safe • having a drink • tourist menus • tipping in hotels • sand • toilets • nudism • suntan • sun cream • souvenirs 1 • souvenirs 2: bumper stickers • local alcohol • local produce • holiday insurance scams • 'officials' • foreign policemen • Customs and Excise officers • Do they hate us? They certainly do • language

RETURNING HOME 189

INTRODUCTION

Cliff Richard – no, wait! come back! – once sang, 'We're all going on a summer holiday / No more worries for a week or two.' Cliff, or his lyricist, must have never been on holiday before that song was written, because if they had, the song would have run, 'We're all going on a summer holiday / Constant worry for a week or two / Not to mention a huge financial loss, massive delays at Heathrow airport and some abject misery'. In the movie, Cliff and his pals drive a London bus through Europe. In reality, if they'd had any sense, they would have driven a tank.

Holidays are terrible things. They are not 'relaxing'. They are not 'fun'. They are awful. The people who say, 'Phew! I need a holiday to

The Great British holiday; like the D-Day landings with donkeys.

9

get over that holiday!' are not telling half the story. 'I need six months of complete rest plus a blood transfusion and fifty thousand pounds compensation' would be nearer the mark.

From the moment you close your front door, wondering if all your plants will die and if you have left the gas on, to your arrival at an overcrowded airport staffed by people who hate you because you are going away and they have to work here, to your actual stay in some incomplete, lizard-ridden prison camp for sunbeds, there will be no respite. You will not relax. You will not have fun. You will not even be able to lounge by the pool because a) there is a dead mongoose in it, and b) there will be the Germans.

Deep down, we know holidays are not good. In the year 2000 the Trading Standards Institute received 12,551 complaints from people

'Flight 456 is late again, George.'

who'd had vile holidays. A year later that figure had risen, amazingly, to 28,502. At this rate, by next Tuesday over 50,000 people a year are having holidays that are so bad they are compelled to complain to someone about them.

It's true that we all like to complain. We are ingenious in our efforts. In a recent report from something called the European Consumer Centre, 10,000 people had a righteous go at holidays. True, one pair of holidaymakers complained about the lack of potatoes in Rome. Admittedly, someone else was upset because he had booked a skiing holiday but when he arrived at the resort there was no snow. But why not? Surely we expect snow on a skiing trip. And where have the Romans hidden all the spuds?

We live on a cold, damp, wet island. We are entitled to get off it and go somewhere nice. In 2003, 15 million Brits went abroad. We spent nearly 30 billion quid abroad. And what do we get? Toilets that don't work. Food that we can't spell. And foreigners who don't like us. Foreigners are a major part of holidays. They live there, and they pretend they want us to visit. 'Come to our country!' they insist. 'Bring money!' they mean.

And they do not understand our culture. They think we like warm beer, football, Shakespeare and the Middle Ages. This is true. The Frequently Asked Questions section of a major website for Americans visiting the UK contains the query: 'Can tourists bring bows and arrows into Britain?' (The answer, brilliantly, was 'There are currently no restrictions on the importation of archery equipment into Britain.') On one site, a Czech woman says of British 'booze tourists': 'It's disgusting. The British don't know when to stop. They drink and drink and drink.' And a Polish site for visitors to Britain contains this information about seaside holidays: 'Older adults are happy just to sit in their deck-chairs and occasionally go for a paddle with their skirts or trouser legs hitched up. The water is always cold and sometimes very dirty.'

As for the British abroad, the Polish traveller is told that 'In fact, about 40% of the population do not go away anywhere for their holidays.' Our own Office of National Statistics is more specific; that

40% is in fact the over-65s. The really big holiday-making group are those of us aged 45 to 54. And this in spite of the fact that, according to the same statistics, the 45 to 54 age group are some of the most grumpy people in the country, and the least likely to have a decent time abroad. It's true. With our dislike of change, travel, hot weather and having to speak foreign, us grumpy folk make very unlikely holidaymakers. If a grumpy person sends a postcard, when we write 'Wish you were here,' the unspoken missing word is 'instead'.

This book is for the unwilling traveller, the natural stay-at-home who has been somehow forced to go away from home, the reluctant tourist, and the person for whom the journey through life is bad enough, let alone the journey through customs – in short, the grumpy old man on holiday.

David Quantick

PLANNING THE THING

PRE-HOLIDAY GLOOM

A̲ll work and no play makes Jack a dull boy. Bully for Jack, eh? Some work and no play makes the rest of us go barmy. All work and no play would cause the nation to rise up as one and throw whole offices into the briny deep. Work is a horrible thing, designed by people who have accidentally purchased factories or cubicles in bulk, and need other people to be in them. If you have failed to win the Lottery or inherit Salford, there is only one escape that does not involve a bottle of sleeping pills. A holiday.

Unfortunately, you have a job. And, despite the fact that the boss claims regularly that some hair could do your job in its sleep, you are not allowed to just walk out of the building saying, 'I'm off on

It's only a picture.

holiday. Tell the hair to keep out of my desk drawer.' No, you have to get time off.

Things have improved since the old days. In the old days, it used to be like this:

'Hello, I'd like some time off.'

'Would you now? You're sacked.'

'Oh.'

Now it is a lot better:

'Hello, I'd like some time off.'

'All right then.'

'Thanks.'

'Oh, if you pull a stunt like this again, we'll outsource all your projects and hotdesk them in from York.'

'Tangeriney.'

And now we are in the EU we do not get such bad paid holidays as we used to. No, we are right up there with Belorussia and Bosnia-Herzegovina. The world is your oyster, except you can't afford any oysters, not if you want to go on holiday as well.

TRAVEL SHOWS
∾

Supposedly these things exist to give us holiday ideas. Certainly they give us the chance to shout rude things at tangerine-faced TV presenters as they sit under a beach brolly somewhere nice looking, relaxed and overpaid. But beware. We all sense that travel shows are fixed, that the tangeriney presenters do not have two kids and a hard-drinking spouse to tow around, and that they only go for two days with a camera crew, a limo and a six-star hotel to repair to each evening. But the truth is much worse. Like the Moon landings, all travel shows are faked on a back lot in a film studio, free from mosquitoes, rug-sellers and Germanically towelled sunbeds. Probably.

And all the programme-makers are on a backhander from a crooked travel company.

BROCHURES
∾

Beautiful books of lies. The weather is better in the photos. The sea is cleaner. Hotels are shinier and newer than in real life. As are the people. The tourists in the brochure are sleeker, fitter and substantially less hefty than the people you will meet on your actual holiday. This is because they are professional models, not German accountants and Turkish lady shot-putters.

On the cruise ship two grey-haired holidaymakers in matching white look at the lights on the fast-approaching shore, unaware that they are not festive neon, but rather burning buildings.

At least they finished the brochure on time.

The things they are doing are lies, too. The couple racing each other into the sea will stop at the shoreline, before tumbling into a murky surf full of broken bottles, fish floating on their backs, and pre-owned marital aids. The beautiful blonde waving at her friends from the water is trying to summon help because she's got her foot trapped in a submerged supermarket trolley. And the family enjoying a beach barbecue are turning down the heat to avoid igniting a nearby oil spill.

Meanwhile in Austria white-toothed young skiers pose on a hillside whose main source of photographic whiteness is Tipp-Ex rather than snow. In far-off South America a family joke with a waiter who is less interested in taking their order than finding out how much ransom he can get if he kidnaps them all. On the cruise ship two grey-haired holidaymakers in matching white look at the lights on the fast-approaching shore, unaware that they are not festive neon, but rather burning buildings.

BROCHURES 2
∾

That's before you get to 'Prices and Availability'. These are best read as beautiful poems rather than actual guides to cost and booking options. The price of a hotel room has apparently been mixed up with the price of hiring a sunbed, as it is some fourteen times lower than it will be when your credit card bill arrives. Air fares in the brochure would not vex the Wright Brothers, but in reality relate more to the cost of sending 100 men to the Moon.

As for availability... brochures have their own upside-down logic. In the world of the sane, peak periods are the busiest, and therefore the hardest to book during, while the quiet periods – the middle of winter, say, or blizzard season – are when there will be rooms aplenty.

But in Brochure World the opposite pertains. You want a room off-season, when it's – and the clue is in this word – cheap? There aren't any. Well, there were yesterday, and if you'd called at four a.m. this morning... but they've all gone. For some mysterious reason, even though it's freezing and the beach is ten foot deep in snow and fallen leaves, there are all of a sudden no rooms. This is provable via mathematical formula: x being the amount of cheap rooms, y being the demand, and x times $y = 0$.

So you are forced to take a room at the height of the season. And even though the world and his wife, and their kids and their granny, have all descended on the tiny resort of Tinymalinos, where there are only two hotels and a shed, there is a plethora of rooms available. They just happen to cost… well, whatever your annual salary is, multiplied by five. Funny, that.

TRAVEL BROCHURE JARGON

Palm-fringed beach – beggar-fringed beach
Stone's throw from the beach – if that stone was being fired from a supercannon
Sun-drenched – drenched
Golden sands – glass-strewn
Family-run – Mafia-run
We would strongly recommend hiring a car – We would strongly recommend sleeping in it, too.
Self-catering – The restaurant burnt down last year.

ONLINE BOOKING

All the fun of brochures, only worse. The reason that the '360 degree shot' of the hotel room only goes round 180 degrees is because the half of the room you can't see has a stripped-down World War II motorbike and sidecar in the corner. The short video of the breathtaking Cretan mountain scene cuts out just before you can examine the hillside dappled with old washing machines and busted fridges. And the counter at the bottom does not indicate 23,583 happy visitors, but rather 23,583 angry people looking for the 'Contact Us' button because there isn't a 'Take Legal Action against Us' button.

But far more evil than all of these things is the booking section.

Once upon a time, booking a holiday went like this:

'Hello, I'd like to book a skiing holiday in Norway. Two people, for two weeks, starting on December the 2nd.'

'Certainly, sir. That'll be ten guineas.'

And that was the end of it. Nowadays you can book online, for added convenience. Here is a short guide to booking online:

After much waiting, the form appears on screen. You type in your name and email address.

Time passes. The screen lazily re-forms itself. It tells you, 'You are not registered,' and you have to start again.

You type in your name. Twice, in case the tour company thinks you might have forgotten how to spell it, or, like Shakespeare, you favour many variant spellings.

You hit Return. This time the screen tells you, 'There is an account already open in this name.' You vaguely recall trying to book a holiday with this company a year ago and giving up in frustration and blind rage.

To avoid confusion, you select a new login name, and continue to the second box. Now they want a password. You type in a suitable memorable but unusual word.

Immediately the screen flashes up, 'This password has been taken.' Given that the word you took for your password was GRENWADDLE, this seems extraordinary. Your next four selections – HUMPWILLOCK, TONKERS, VLADIMONKEY and OLD MOTHER CHITTERS – are also rejected.

The computer suggests a password for you. It is, memorably, 27DHC95NFUQ9XSNIGJAK. You accept, and are then asked to put in a 'Password Reminder' to help jog your memory if, by some fluke, you cannot commit 27DHC95NFUQ9XSNIGJAK to memory.

You cannot think of anything that would remind you of 27DHC95NFUQ9XSNIGJAK, so you type in 'What my password is'.

This logical loop so upsets your computer that it crashes, and you

The computer suggests a password for you. It is, memorably, 27DHC95NFUQ9XSNIGJAK.

have to start all over again, again. You take a break and think about making a holiday checklist instead.

HOLIDAY CHECKLISTS
↬

These are absolutely crucial. Year after year the same list, with minor variations for climate, etc. (see *What to pack in …*), will serve the traveller well. You cannot go wrong with a holiday checklist. Which is probably why no one ever makes one. A week before the holiday somebody will say, 'We must make a list of things to take.' A few days later, in the middle of dinner, someone will say, 'Ooh! First aid box,' and then carry on eating. The day before leaving, while packing (see *Packing*), someone else will say, 'Did anyone make a list?' Someone else will say, 'I thought you were going to do it.' And then there will be a huge ruck.

Anybody thinking of making a holiday checklist (as distinct from actually making a checklist, which has never happened) will want to include at least one of the following items:

First Aid box

You think you've got one. Or rather, you remember seeing a sort of red tin with a cross on it somewhere. Or is it green? Anyway, you've got one. Upon investigation, you discover that you haven't. You go into town to buy one, but there aren't any, except in the specialist camping shop, which sells a super de luxe First Aid box with mosquito nets, water-purifying tablets and a defibrillator. Weighing cost against use, you decide not to buy it as you're only going to Thanet. On the first day, you get bitten by a mosquito while drinking some polluted water and have a small heart attack.

Torch

Who needs a torch? You do. All holidays involve at least one five-minute journey in total darkness through an unfamiliar area, whether it's unpacking a tent in a dark field (see *Camping*), trying to find a holiday cottage at 3 a.m. (see *Holiday cottages*) or just trying to have a pee behind a Hungarian railway station in a power cut (see *Inter-railing*). This is when you will break your leg.

Batteries

For the torch. And for every other thing you have brought with you, since you forgot to get the foreign adaptor plugs.

> **Now that people on the Continent have the euro, and the internet, and flushing toilets, it doesn't seem too much for them to get proper plugs.**

Foreign adaptor plugs

Now that people on the Continent have the euro, and the internet, and flushing toilets, it doesn't seem too much for them to get proper plugs. Three sturdy prongs is obviously what nature intended a plug to have, not two tiny ski poles for ants. Then again, when you actually manage to get the telly or radio going, you wonder why you bothered.

Water

They have water abroad, you cry. You're staying in a four-star hotel, for goodness' sake. It's perfectly safe to drink, well, sometimes. Yes, but it tastes of flower wee.

Washing kit

Again, surely you can pick up these things abroad? Not so. Despite the fact that foreign countries dominate the market in toiletries – all those chic French perfumes, soaps and body products – when you nip into the local *pharmacie* or *Toilettenprodukterei*, all they have is something in a tube that is a pinky-yellow and apparently called Pshifiss or something that a 9-year-old boy will find hilarious.

So stock up. Empty the bathroom. Otherwise you will find yourself at a caravan site near Santander naked and shouting, 'Has anyone got any Pshifiss?' at 6 in the morning.

Travel wash

A special shampoo for clothes which enables you to do your laundry on holiday in a hand basin. Tip: Save money and packing time and use actual shampoo. It will smell no worse and will ensure your socks don't get dandruff.

Travel iron

Really, don't bother. They are so small that you won't need one unless you are going abroad to an Action Man convention and you think his trousers might need pressing.

Toilet roll

For when the *Daily Mail* is not enough.

Suntan lotion

It may rain all holiday long, but you need to take something that will leak all over the clothes in your suitcase.

ONLINE BOOKING 2

After abandoning your holiday checklist, you go online again. The computer makes you go through all the previous steps one more time and then suddenly comes up with an actual booking form. You fill in as many details as possible without swearing, repeating hundreds of small facts and going back a lot to put in small facts that they insist are essential. A red star next to one space indicates that someone, somewhere, is insistent on having your wife's mobile phone number.

At last, a real question. 'Which flight do you wish to take?' Not having a timetable for Stinkska Airlines to hand, you try to open a website for Stinkska Airlines. The booking form vanishes and you have to start again.

The only flight available gets in at 4 a.m. Your connection to the resort is at 9 p.m. the same day. Oh well. Trying not to think of how you and yours will pass an entire day in the confines of Oxtermerkin

Airport, you forge on. It is getting dark outside. You have foolishly decided to do all this on a work computer, and Hipkiss from Accounts is giving you frowny looks.

A little padlock appears to alert internet fraudsters to the fact that some fool is using their credit card online. You are now being asked for your credit card details. 'What is the name on your card?' You resist the urge to put 'Biggles' and type in the same name that you have typed everywhere else, i.e. your own bloody name.

Several minutes pass and you are returned to the top of the page. It appears that your name is not your name. This is because on your credit card you used your full name, which includes your middle name, which is something awful like Lislebert or Shimping.

You type in your embarrassing middle name, start date and expiry date. Now you are asked to put in your security number. Next to this request is a button labelled 'What is my security number?'. This strikes you as a very good question, so you click the button, which tells you that the security number is on the back of your card.

You look at your card. There isn't a security number. You raise the keyboard to your head and beat it against your forehead until the O key falls off. Then you get out a different card, the one you promised the wife you would use only in an emergency, but which does at least have a security number.

Finally! 'Tickets will be sent to the above address.' Confusingly, two addresses appear. One is slightly wrong and the other, weirdly, is that of your psychotic ex-girlfriend.

You correct the address and hit 'Continue'. You are nearly done. 'How did you hear about us?' the screen asks. After looking unsuccessfully for an answer that says 'Satan told me about it', you hit 'Other' and then 'Click to confirm booking.'

The screen empties. There is a company logo, and underneath it, nothing. The screen stares at you, blinking, as if to say, 'Who the hell are you?' You throw the computer at Hipkiss from Accounts and go to the travel agent instead.

HOLIDAY INSURANCE

❧

The golden rule of holiday insurance is, of course, that if you have got it – that is, if you have given lots of money to some crooks in an office – you will not need it. Your holiday will be a creamy glide through health, fun and comfort. If you have not got holiday insurance, you will be set upon by footpads the moment you get abroad, and will then catch the plague on the way to casualty.

JABS AND PILLS

❧

'Hi! I'm going on a much-needed holiday to a hot foreign land.' 'Excellent – here, I'm going to stick not one but many needles in you. You'll feel sick and have to take the day off work, and then you'll have to come back again and have some more needles stuck in you. Then there's mosquitoes.'

'What about mosquitoes?'

A McDonald's for mosquitoes.

'Oh, don't worry, there's a choice. You can have injections whose side-effects include dizziness, nausea, headaches, vomiting, blindness, the trots and hair loss, or an overpriced course of tablets which have no side-effects because they're actually old mints.'

'Maybe I'll just go to Rhyl instead.'

TRAVEL AGENTS

A hole in time, a window into an earlier era, the travel agent is where you should take your kids if ever they ask you what the 1970s were like. From the dusty model airliner in the window, decorated in the livery of some long-defunct Central European airline, to the sun-damaged posters that have now faded to a watery blue so you can't tell if they're meant to be a beach or a mountain, travel agents are depressing islands of history. They are leftovers from

The golden age of travel: when BOAC flew thrice monthly to Skegness.

A window into an earlier era, the travel agent is where you should take your kids if ever they ask you what the 1970s were like.

a time when booking a holiday meant going into town, sitting in front of a little desk and talking to someone for several hours. After which they would get on the phone and call someone in another office and, occasionally covering the phone with their hand, hint strongly that they would 'sort you something good out'. They never did, unless 'something good' was travel agent slang for 'Dubrovnik in February'.

Now the world has changed. Dubrovnik is no longer in Yugoslavia (nor is anything else). Travel agents no longer get on the blower, or if they do it's on some pointless headset thing which enables them to talk to someone else while staring blankly into the middle of your face. But the dusty airliner is still in the window, and the posters are still bluely incomprehensible, and the essential travel agent attitude is still in place.

For you, booking a holiday is a means to an end. For them, it's a sort of cross between poker and Twenty Questions. They hold the cards – the phone headset thing, the computer – and they know all the answers.

'We'd like to go to Barcelona in May.'

'We haven't anything in Barcelona in May.'

'Does that mean you have nothing in May? Or does it mean you have nothing in Barcelona?'

'Not necessarily.'

'All right then, do you have something in Barcelona but not in May?'

'Maybe.'

'Aha! Then would I be right in saying that you do not have something in May but you do have something in Barcelona.'

'Yes! Damn! Oh, wait… it's gone.'

And so on.

WHAT HOLIDAY?

FAMILY HOLIDAYS

The image of a family holiday, as enshrined in Ladybird books and wartime propaganda films, is a delightful one, the family car crammed with buckets and spades, suitcases strapped to the roof rack, the wife with her headscarf on and the kids reading the *Dandy* on the back seat. St Austell here we come!

In reality, one of the main reasons you actually want a holiday is to get away from the family. Unfortunately, you can't say, 'Well, I'm off

Daddy's suitcase is very heavy. It is full of whisky bottles.

on my holiday. Bye.' That's called a trial separation and nobody wants a custody battle just because they fancied a couple of nights in Bruges. So the only solution is to take them with you. This does reduce some tensions, but introduces others. However, there is nothing you can do. You may vaguely hope they'll say they don't want you with them, so they can go on holiday and you can spend two weeks in the pub. And in fact, they hope you'll say you don't want them with you so they can go on a nice holiday without that miserable git ruining it for them.

In the end, everyone goes on holiday together to preserve the family unit, which means that ten minutes after loading the car you will be reflecting deeply on the many possible other meanings of the phrase 'nuclear family'. The main cause of this increasingly tense reflection will be the smaller passengers in the back seat. Young passengers have few ambitions. They would like a cheeseburger. They would like to watch a DVD. They would like to be sick. But most of all, they would like to see the sea. No matter that you have shelled out many big ones on a skiing holiday, or a visit to the Negev Desert. All they want to do is see the sea and then chant, 'I can see the sea! I can see the sea!' over and over again. While they are doing this, take time off from cursing the linguistic coincidence that makes 'see' and 'sea' so tempting to the chant-maker, and instead steel yourself for the inevitable rondelay of 'Are we nearly there yet?'

There is one way to prevent a prolonged bout of 'Are we nearly there yet?' and that is to pre-empt the whole vile business by inventing your own chant called 'Are we still bloody miles away?' Kids will go mental for it.

HONEYMOONS

Honeymoons are the, well, honeymoon period of marriage. This is because, unlike much married life, honeymoons are short, involve a lot of sex, and take place somewhere nice.

Honeymoons used to be, frankly, the first occasion a young married couple would have sex. Nowadays, in a world where most people have sex with each other within ten seconds of meeting, a honeymoon has to offer something more than the promise of clumsy rumpo. Therefore young marrieds find that a hotel room in Cleethorpes loses its appeal after the first hour or so, and begin to wish that they had gone somewhere more interesting, like Morecambe Bay, or Venice.

Young marrieds who do go somewhere more interesting find that they cannot resist the urge to tell fellow tourists they are on honeymoon and, after a barrage of 'Honeymoon, eh? Surprised you've got the strength to leave the room,' wish that they had gone somewhere quieter, like Cleethorpes, or Venus.

Ultimately, alas, all honeymoons are doomed because of what one expert calls 'the whole "it's got to be perfect" syndrome', which is not a compulsion to hear the music of Fairground Attraction, but rather the desire shared by bride and groom that, as this is not only their first holiday as a married couple but also the final instalment of their perfect wedding, nothing must go wrong. There cannot be a better way of ensuring that everything that can go wrong does go wrong.

No need to travel abroad to tie the knot. Global warming means you can now have a beach wedding in sunny, only-slightly-polluted Redcar.

These people are lucky they don't get kidnapped and thrown into a South American jail with that attitude. And that's only if they take their honeymoon in the Lake District.

The only way for a honeymoon couple to avoid disappointment is to build disappointment into the honeymoon. Book a week in a Portakabin next to a slagheap. Take the mother-in-law. Walk into pubs and insult the locals. You may come home cold, smelly, annoyed and worked-over, but you won't be disappointed and you will, in a way, have achieved some sort of perfection.

INTER-RAILING

This is the chance to be poor in seventeen different countries. Inter-railing is based on the idea that young, fit and idealistic people can travel around Europe cheaply on special railcards. They have to be young, fit and idealistic because anybody else would be done in by the experience. Never mind that these perky young student types will be exposed to the horror of Europe's railway

Inter-railing is the chance to be poor in seventeen different countries.

stations, dens of iniquity the lot of them, or that they will waste hours of their lives sitting on a tiny platform at Interlachen waiting for the 04.23 to Crimpen Dorfbogger. Leave aside the entire day spent trapped in a tiny compartment with a 95-year-old Swiss peasant who wants to tell you his life story in the dialect of his village. And try not to consider the joys of Italian passport control (demand passport while brandishing machine gun, open passport, look at photo, laugh heartily). The worst part of inter-railing is trying to get out of Britain on a train. Five hours on Virgin Rail would bring back happy memories for any frequent pre-war Albanian train user.

But the real reason to go inter-railing is to accumulate a mental library of experiences, memories and unforgettable moments – a library that you can refer to in later life, so you know never to do anything like that again. The best thing about inter-railing is that it makes bad hotels and unpleasant plane journeys seem somehow much nicer.

What could be better designed to promote harmony between nations than student exchange holidays? War, frankly, among other things.

STUDENT EXCHANGE HOLIDAYS

∾

This was one of the many community-minded ideas of the 1950s, like collective farming and nuclear power plants, which never worked quite so well in real life. Student exchange holidays were a simple idea: you go to a foreign land and stay with a foreign lad or lass the same age as you, and then they come and stay with you. What could be easier and better designed to promote harmony between nations? War, frankly, among other things.

Student exchanges are fraught with difficulty. For a start, the foreign kid either speaks immaculate English, which means you are lumbered with a swot for two weeks, or else they speak no English, which means you are lumbered with a weeping teenager who makes international phone calls in weepy foreign to *les parents* three times a day. You also get a strange doubling of all the problems that occur when groups of teenagers are brought together: twice as much fighting, double the sulking, and 100 per cent increase in acne'd sexual tension.

It is hard to say which is worse, the visit abroad (you can't speak the language, the food tastes weird, and you have never been in a foreign house before) or the return visit (your friends prefer your exchange partner, they smoke dope in the front room, your little sister teaches them ten essential four-letter words). Either way, they are a bad idea. Should you be a teenager reading this who has been 'offered the chance' to go on one of these exchanges, suggest to your parents that they swap places with the foreign mum and dad first. See how rarely the foreign exchange visit is mentioned after this.

BACKPACKING 1

∾

The name suggests a kind of human snail, home on his or her back, just kinda truckin' across Europe, no fixed ideas, maybe meeting some interesting people, hanging out in some unusual places and, you know, like fending for themselves. The reality is hard and different. It is a big weeping lad in a phone box in Utrecht, trying to get his mum to 'wire' 5,000 euros over, when neither of them know what 'wire' exactly means, and if his dad finds out he'll go mental. It is three nice girls from York wondering how quickly they can leave a boarding house in Santander that is apparently run

Quick! Creep up and steal their enormous possessions!

by some Spanish cousins of the Manson family. And it is a flaming Italian tourist stood at Oxford Circus turning round slowly to look at the top of the Niketown building so that his bag of useless travel crap keeps slapping everyone in the head.

They are travelling the world cheaply, by not staying in hotels and instead spending each night in a Dettol-smelling hostel. This means they have to cart their weird possessions round in the daytime in a stupid camper's satchel. All to 'save money'. Here's a way of saving money. Don't buy a sodding backpack. And if you do, don't fill it with useless old toot. The whole point, surely, of backpacking is that it's a carefree amble around the world, unburdened with luggage and material possessions. Not a nice day out for your satchel.

> **Why are they always looking up? There is no information above ten feet anywhere except on motorways.**

Backpackers are the bane of modern life. You can't go three yards without one of them poking you in the eye as they try and work out how far Trafalgar Square is from Nelson's Column. You can't get a seat in the pub because they've put their stupid backpacks on the seats. You can't buy a drink without one of them spilling it with their backpack. They are, in short, awful people and should be stuffed into their own bags and sent home in the hold of a very cheap cargo plane.

BACKPACKING 2
∾

And why are they always looking up? There is no information above ten feet anywhere except on motorways. They must be looking up because they're too stupid to look down, or around, or straight in front. 'I wonder where the zoo is. Perhaps if I stand here for half an hour looking at a cloud, its location will come to me.' *Get out of the way, you luggage-abusing bumcrisis!*

BACKPACKING 3

∼

And how come they're supposed to be these roving free spirits but the only places you ever see backpackers are in McDonald's and Starbucks? And not even McDonald's and Starbucks in out-of-the-way places, either, but in the biggest cities in the world? Come on! Be culturally diverse! What is the point of going halfway round the world just to have the same coffee you could have at home? *Or are you homesick, you great big weeping failed explorer?*

HITCH-HIKING

∼

Hitch-hikers are constantly being advised of the perils of asking total strangers for a ride, and rightly so. Yet who considers the danger for the driver? Not the danger of being robbed, as most hitchers couldn't rob a mannequin with a million euros stapled to it, nor murdered (they're all vegetarians), but of being annoyed to death. The mythic image of hitch-hiking, from the hitch-hiker's point of view, is that of a kind of *On the Road*-type quest, wherein one meets a variety of quirky characters, who add to the hitcher's spiritual development and make him or her a more sorta interesting and poetical kinda creative artist, thing. The image of the hitcher from the driver's point of view is a sunburned geography student on a gap year who has spent the money his parents gave him on marijuana and snowboarding lessons, and is filled with the urge to tell his tiresome holiday stories to someone who cannot get away. Trapped in your car, with Tris the student banging on hour after hour about the time he met these brilliant Goth girls halfway up the Matterhorn and they had, like, this blow, only it was totally legal, is a form of hell that few can survive.

There's a reason hitch-hikers use their thumbs to flag down vehicles. If they used their conversation, no one would ever stop.

WALKING HOLIDAYS

Mankind has devoted thousands of years to inventing ways of not having to walk everywhere. Now we have jets and spacecraft and skateboards and rocket-packs, what do people do for fun? They walk. And not just to the pub or to the car (which is OK and maybe even good for you) but really walking a lot, up hills and, equally literally, down dales. Some people think the height of pleasure is to walk miles and sodding miles through bog and mountain dressed as a physics teacher on his day off. They are weird in the head.

It wouldn't be so bad if these people kept their weirdness to themselves, but they have to let us know all about it in a kind of 'Look at me! I'm weird!' sort of way. So they form organizations devoted to walking. What's the point? 'Hello. Let's all meet in a field

And stay there.

and start walking.' You hardly need an organization to do that. They call themselves things like The Ramblers' Association, an apt name given that rambling is normally an activity associated with people who are a bit dull, or even weak in the head. But these ramblers are not merely talking arse the live-long day, they are walking it. They bang on about ancient pathways, when the point is surely that if a pathway is ancient it's going to be not much cop for walking on. They get annoyed when farmers try and stop them going on their land but would presumably kick up a hell of a fuss if some farmers turned up and walked through their physics lessons. And they make a point of dully going on and on about closing gates and picking up litter. Like everyone else thinks we should leave gates open so the cows can go round updating their crisp packet collection.

Ramblers. Tossers would be a better word.

CYCLING HOLIDAYS
∽

'After a day's cycling we are treated to a seemingly endless supply of vegetarian food.' This real quote from a cycling holiday brochure indicates more than mere photographs the true nature of cycling holidays. And they're not even complaining. They're not saying, 'My god, these bastards are trying to kill us.' They're saying, 'Tofu – ooh la la.'

Cycling holidays are bad. For a start, what business does any person born after 1900 have getting on a bicycle in the first place? Are they in the French Resistance? Do they come from a parallel world where cars weren't invented? Have they become obsessed with the novels of Enid Blyton? And even if they have to use a bike, why must they dress like that? Lycra is best left to former members of

Cyclists are barmy. Their dream is a world where vehicles are banned, except for thin metal ones with stupid ding-ee bells that some pillock in a lycra nutcrusher is riding on the pavement.

Pan's People, and wearing those weird jerkins and hats doesn't make you go any faster, unless you have to get to work in exactly 14.00053 seconds every day.

Cyclists are barmy. Their dream is a world where vehicles are banned, except for thin metal ones with stupid ding-ee bells that some pillock in a lycra nutcrusher is riding on the pavement. They want to force this dream upon the entire world, and trundle smugly through the Auvergne or the Pyrenees on what are essentially castrated mopeds. Oddly, they never seem to extend their bikepartheid (it's a word now) onto planes, trains, boats, Volvo estates, or any of the other big petrol-gargling fellows that transport their stupid PC Plod frames around the world.

The cycling holiday is not right. Apart from all that force-feeding them vegetarian food, the holidays are all in not right places. Snowdonia – great place for a bike ride. Hadrian's Wall – that's just surreal. And even a tour of castles in rural Germany suggests that deep down there is something of *Chitty Chitty Bang Bang* about the whole thing.

ACTIVITY HOLIDAYS

This is pretty much an oxymoron. 'Activity' is what we take 'holidays' to get away from. Holidays are things where we do anti-activities like lying down, sleeping, reading, pretending to read, and having a lunch called beer. But activity holidays exist, and are so popular that special activity holiday places have to be built, thereby ruining perfectly good scrapyards and wasteland. Some fool will come along, clear a big bit of land, and build a river through it. Then there will be canoes, for people to tip over and drown in. There will be walks in the woods, which have appeared from nowhere. Cycle trails (see *Cycling holidays*). Dry ski slopes (see *Skiing*). Running tracks. Who goes running on holiday? Mad people and fugitives, that's who.

These holidays are designed, basically, to make you feel that you are not on holiday. They are supposed to give you a sense of achievement. The only sense of achievement they do give you is a sense of having given someone hundreds of pounds just to get you more knackered than you were before you went. The only real reason people take them is because they've got kids, and they know that by sending the little chaps off to exercise themselves stupid they'll be so completely exhausted come the evening it'll give you and yours some time to yourself. Putting rum in their Sunny Delight has the same effect, and is easier.

CLIMBING HOLIDAYS
⌒

Never trust any activity where the guide is prepared to cut a rope to let you fall to your death in order to 'save the others'. Here's a tip: Get him to cut the rope about ten yards from the hotel so you can roll back down the slope and spend the rest of the holiday in Base Camp, i.e. the bar.

Climbing holidays are spectacularly pointless. They are based on the idea of recreating daring, but pointless, mountain climbing exploits of yore. These are the kind of climbs where some public school bloke with a beard takes a week to climb a mountain, loses three colleagues, six toes, a yak, and when asked why he did it, says, 'Because it's there.' Which is the kind of dozy explanation that suits any, or no, situation. 'Why did you drink out of the toilet, Sir Evelyn?' 'Because it's there.'

And so, when somebody asks you why you have wasted two weeks of your life climbing a mountain that has been climbed to pieces already, you can fix them with a noble gaze and say, 'Because it's still there.'

SAGA HOLIDAYS
⌒

Named, for no known reason, after the stories the Vikings told each other of battles with monsters, long journeys that end in conflict, and other things that we like to associate with holidays. Saga holidays are the vacation bookend to Club 18–30. (Club 80–Whenever God Takes Me has less of a ring to it.) The worst thing about them is the advertising, which invariably features two 50 years-olds greyed up to

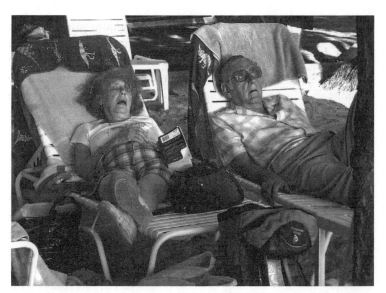

Age and glamour combine in the smooth luxury of a Saga holiday.

look more pensionable lounging about on the deck of a liner, drinking champagne and beaming like they've already lost their marbles. This campaign suggests that when we get older, we become genial souls, smiling benignly at the world through a haze of Dom Perignon and Steradent. This could not be further from the truth. Age brings, not wisdom, but arthritis, rheumatism and a growing belief that the world is run by halfwits who should be thrown into a canyon. Put that in an advert, Saga Holidays.

BEACH RESORT HOLIDAYS

Upon arrival, it seems a very paradise. White sand, blue waves, golden sun. And everything is laid on. You don't have to go outside to eat local food, there's a self-service cantina. The bar serves many cheap drinks of the world. There's a disco and a shop. You can spend the whole holiday within the confines of the resort. In fact,

There is no RSPCA for humans.

you have to, because they won't let you out. The resort is fifteen miles away from the nearest town, the buses are too dangerous to use, and getting a taxi means ordering it from 'reception', which is a local word meaning 'the brother of the cab firm's owner, who owes him 50,000 euros and is trying to get it by ripping off tourists'.

You will spend two weeks eating the same warmed-up fake ethnic gloop, drinking the same badly made watery cocktails, thinking about buying the same tacky souvenirs, and reading the same one and only book you brought with you on the same beach with the same other 500 people.

It's like being in *The Prisoner*, only without the possible frisson of being tongued by a giant balloon. Oh, and it might rain. A lot. All day and all night. All the time. And unlike in the olden days of seaside boarding houses, there's no Ludo under the bench seat.

The danger of rain may be the reason so many beach paradise activities involve getting wet – water-skiing, snorkelling, scuba-

The average beach resort is like being in *The Prisoner*, only without the possible frisson of being tongued by a giant balloon.

diving, paragliding and so forth. Anybody who takes a wetsuit on a beach holiday is not preparing themselves for a week of activity fun, they're admitting defeat before they've even started.

It's almost certain that at some stage on a beach holiday you'll be persuaded to try *scuba-diving*. This is very scary indeed. Proper scuba-divers include men who dive for bits of broken ships, close friends of Flipper, and various shoals of baddies in James Bond films. None of this sounds like much fun, especially if Flipper is having an off day, and this is because scuba-diving is designed to be Not Fun At All.

For a kick-off, you have to undergo a training course, during which you will be told repeatedly that you may actually die while diving, or even training. And you have to sign a release form absolving them of any guilt should you now go out and be eaten by a clam.

So you have spent three whole days of your holiday working, in short, and being reminded of your own mortality. Bet you wish you'd gone snorkelling instead.

Scuba-divers – the ones who do not drown – are particularly annoying company, by the way. They refer to themselves as 'divers', in case 'scuba' sounds a bit weedy, and they draw attention to their underwater foolishness by calling their flippers 'fins'. They are, in short, the reason God made sharks.

One way to avoid the bends and the expense while cutting out the middle man is to eat three dinners, and, when the indigestion kicks in, stick your head in the fish tank. It may be unpleasant, but at least it's free, and it'll stop you nicking the last few remaining bits of coral we have left.

Or go *snorkelling*. It's just as much fun, it requires a lot less silly frogman clothing, and best of all, if you've had a couple of drinks before you go in, you can swim about talking to the fish by making 'oggle boggle' noises through your mouthpiece.

600 quid the lessons cost him and he's going to get his money's worth.

It's your worst nightmare... a nudist with transport.

SAILING HOLIDAYS

~

There are many kinds of sailing holiday, but the two most annoying are the yachty kind and the big clipper kind. The yachty kind is not too bad, in that you get to sit around inside a very nice aquatic hotel and drink cocktails with fat billionaires. Unfortunately, the chances of being invited on one of these are fairly low unless you are a fat billionaire or a 'chorus girl'. In which case, you will have to sleep with one or the other.

The big clipper kind of sailing holiday is surprisingly popular, especially with the young, and the gullible. This is because, on paper, it looks ace. Your school or youth award scheme – Hello, the Duke of Edinburgh! – is offering your parents the chance to pay good money for you to spend ten weeks crewing a big proper white sailing ship like in the movies! Sailing the world, or part of it, with a jolly crew of like-minded teens! Seeing dolphins and turtles and whales and other animals that vegetarians think are pretty! And so forth.

In fact, it would be almost preferable to have sex with the fat billionaire than to go on one of these trips. Essentially, these fun-loving youngsters have been tricked by propaganda and lies into becoming someone's free crew for six months. On land, it's a jolly recruitment session with alcopops all round. On board, everyone is herded below decks and locked up until they get used to the noise of the rats. Then back on deck to be shouted at by a man with a pointless beard for several weeks.

All this, they tell the kids, is character building. Nobody has yet explained why characters can only be built by doing unpleasant things to them. Surely it is possible to build a character in pleasant ways, not by feeding the grown-ups of the future biscuits made out of old cork tiles and bread with weevils in it.

In this floating hell, it seems almost cruel to let the kids take the odd day off in desolate harbours called Tierra Tel Morte every four weeks. Why not just chain them all up, fit oars and make them row to the beat of a big drum?

CRUISES
❧

The adverts are all aimed at the elderly, because nobody under 65 can afford to go on the bloody things. And the over-65s are sickened by the adverts, which portray anybody with grey hair as a simpering, senescent gimp whose idea of fun is standing on a deck 200 feet above sea level with another simpering gimp staring at the sunrise. Later, they will be invited to play table flaming tennis or eat a meal which consists, bafflingly, of about a million shrimps arranged in a circle.

Cruise ships are portrayed as floating palaces, homes away from home where hundreds of people glide from port to port, enjoying local culture. In fact, they are enormous litter bins of the ocean, polluting the place like incontinent robot whales, while – bizarre fact – when in port the electricity they generate is powerful enough to disrupt televisions and lights in local buildings. It's like waking up and finding Derby parked next to you.

The idea of seeing the world by ship is a nice one, except you don't see the world, you see the bits of the world near the edges. On an ideal planet designed by cruise companies, all the good towns and sights would be conveniently located by the seaside, and all the unpleasant industrial bits and villages where people who smell live would be far, far inland.

DISNEY
∾

When people are asked what they would do if they had a time machine, most of them say things like, 'I would like to see some dinosaurs,' or 'I see. So I've got to assassinate Hitler, then? It's always Muggins.' But for some of us, if we had a time machine, its special purpose would clearly be to travel back in time to the early twentieth century, and bribe lots of movie critics to say that the cartoon film *Steamboat Willie* was a load of crap. This being Walt Disney's first great hit, and the film that launched that stupid sodding mouse on its voyage of horror. The whole Disney empire would be stopped in its tracks, and we would be spared not only a shipload of godawful cartoons, but also a world of awful theme parks, and a general sense of smuggo global pseudo-Christianity with a naff pubescent moustache. A sentence beginning 'The worst thing about Walt Disney…' can go many, many ways, but for our purposes let us assume that there is some merit in films like *Herbie Rides Again* and *That Darn Cat* and that the worst thing about Walt Disney is, or are, the theme parks.

They are all the same, only slightly different. A collection of desperate actors welcome you in stinking fake animal suits, and you are shoved into a huge park full of concrete models of a pervert's idea

If you find yourself in Disneyland with these two people, pay the one on the left to beat the crap out of the one on the right. Not the other way round.

of history. Wherever you go, distorted and wrong versions of characters from once-great children's stories wave at you and pose for sweaty photos. 'Rides' pop up every now and then, sick attempts to turn films you thought you had erased from your crying mind into equally unpleasant fairground attractions (although, more frighteningly, there are now movies based on the rides, and so, presumably, there are rides based on movies based on rides based on…). The general impression is of a totalitarian rally manned by giant toys.

A few years ago, at Disno-Merde or whatever that vile nightmare factory near Paris is called now, some Frenchmen infiltrated the place dressed as cartoon characters from French culture. This brilliant act of subversion ought to be imitated around the world, only instead of French cartoon characters people should feel free to substitute figures from their own popular mythology, such as the SAS.

CANAL HOLIDAYS

~

What a non-delight! Canals are rivers with Asperger's Syndrome. Rivers are fond of meandering prettily through the countryside, pausing only to hurl themselves over some picturesque rock or donate their energies to being a big old lake. Canals are not. Canals go in straight lines. If things start to get a bit exciting, canals turn into locks and everyone has to get out and calm down. And canals never go anywhere good. True, they might march past the odd country pub or two, but in single file so

Canals are rivers with Asperger's Syndrome.

you can't get off and go and get hammered, you have to keep going on Mr Canal's Overly Regimented Day Out. But generally canals are going one place and one place only, and that is the outskirts of Birmingham. Can there be any grimmer holiday location than going through part of Brum? And not even trendy, downtown Birmingham, or the bit where they've got a superstore made out of bubblewrap. No, canals always go to the unpleasant, tumbleweedy, rust-buggered bit where they used to make heavy things for export.

All of this is excused by canal fans because canals, they explain, were built for commerce, not pleasure. Canals are roads, they tell you. Right. There is a simple retort to this. No they're not. Roads go to interesting places. Nobody ever coined the saying, 'All roads lead to Birmingham.' Canals are unpleasant. (One of the best bits of news for astronomers must be discovering that the planet Mars does not have any canals, and is therefore free of anally retentive rivers full of space prams.)

And yet, despite the purely industrial purpose of canals, people think they are brilliant things to go on holiday along. Why? Nobody goes to spend a week in a disused biscuit factory or goes surfing in a sewage works. But canals are sort of uniquely English (and Dutch) and so it's fun.

Also – oh no! – you can go in a *barge*.

Harrison Ford enjoys England's inland waterways. For some weird reason.

There are ten reasons why barges are evil:

1 You could find yourself suddenly heading for the weir without a reverse gear.
2 Phone and TV connections are non-existent.
3 The feeling of premature burial is inescapable.
4 Someone has painted flowers and an awful name like *Ol' Molly* on the side.
5 There's the possibility of falling off the barge and into the stagnant deep.
6 Other people in barges are clearly red-faced alternative lifestyle nutters.
7 Sting lives on one. Probably.
8 You spend an awful lot of time lying on your back with your feet on the clammy underside of a bridge pushing the barge along.
9 Chemical toilets. Even the image of Sting sitting on his chemical toilet, reading the *Guardian*, cannot make these terrible buckets of blue unpleasantness any better
10 Ow! My head.

CAMPING HOLIDAYS
~

Camping is horrible. Wet, damp and stupid, it is a concept so uncivilized that the French, who fancy themselves when it comes to being civilized, do not have a word for it, and call it '*le camping*'. '*Le wetdampandstupid*' would be a much better word.

From the wigwam of the Native American to the yurt of the Mongolian, tents are the preserve of nomadic peoples, tribes who do not wish to settle down and build cities, but rather wander round following some fat hairy animals and occasionally milking

For a kick-off, you are not allowed to camp anywhere nice. On the beach at St Tropez? Sorry. In Farmer Crime's muddy field? No problem.

They sold a perfectly good house to buy this.

them. Anyone else does not require a tent, especially since the invention of bricks. Tents are very low on the ladder of decent accommodation. They are made of fabric, for a kick-off. Nobody ever built a castle out of fabric. One that didn't inflate, anyway. Bouncy castles apart, the world is distinctly lacking in fabric lighthouses, fabric palaces or fabric museums. Canvas is not the preferred tool of the builder. And so on.

The idea that you might spend the night under canvas if you were trapped halfway up Mount Everest is a fairly sensible one (although you ought really to try and befriend a yeti, or at least shave one). The idea that you might spend the night under canvas in a place where there are houses, and hotels, and even barns, is a ridiculous one. Camping is horrible. Scouts do it. But then they have to. Their motto is 'Be Prepared'. Yours is 'Get a Hotel'.

For a kick-off, you are not allowed to camp anywhere nice. Pitch a tent in the Ritz? Not allowed. On the beach at St Tropez? Sorry. In Farmer Crime's muddy field? No problem. Or you can go to a campsite. Campsites are very special places indeed. Oh, hang – no, they aren't. They're fields. Fields where nothing grows, otherwise Farmer Crime wouldn't be leasing them out by the square yard to poor sods like you. Campsites have no redeeming features, unless a tree that everyone wees under is a redeeming feature (clue: it isn't). Campsites have plenty of unredeeming features, though.

1 The tap in the middle of the field, which drips, and is the only source of drinking water for you, and five billion thirsty flies.
2 The 'shower block', which is basically a disused cowshed that the EU said was unfit for keeping cows in, so now houses five or six sort of shower things. There is no lesser pleasure than being woken up at 5 a.m. by the sound of cows wondering where their shed went, deciding you might as well get up in case you miss one tiny second of misery, and going for a shower. Your bare feet scrape horribly on the manurey concrete floor. Your eyes try not to

Campsites – silent rock festivals.

register the tiny blocks of army soap scattered here and there, the empty Head and Shoulders bottles, and the enormous Dutchman who comes here every year just to take his shower at the same time as you. You shower hastily, realize you have forgotten your towel, and dry yourself on your socks.

3 The 'shop'. This shop reminds you how our ancestors must have lived. Assuming, of course, our ancestors had a thing for beach balls, shrimping nets, cut-price Nat King Cole CDs and bread so white you could print books on it. Any food or drink you buy in this shop will give you spots. Any other items you purchase can only be used on the beach, assuming the wind doesn't smash them or take them bowling away into the distance first.

4 Tents. Other people's tents are better than yours, but do they sit inside them, the nosy beggars? No, they sit outside them playing mah-jong and drinking Brandy Alexanders, while you struggle with something that seemed fine in the shop, but here, now, is a jumble of poles and cloth. Eventually you give up, go into town and buy one of those tents that you just have to take out of the bag and they flip into place. You take it out of the bag, flip it into place, and the wind blows it over the edge of a cliff.

No camping trip is deemed complete without a *campfire singalong*. These are two words that only a talentless musician or an ego-ridden collector of jovial songs could relish. Since the invention of telly – hell, since the invention of reading – singalongs have been rendered pretty pointless. If you really want to hear rotten music outdoors, go down to Woolworths, get some CDs at random from the bargain bin, and play them on the car stereo while parked outside the house.

SKIING HOLIDAYS
∾

'Are you going on the piste?' Shut up. Skiing holidays are very odd things. Marketed as activity holidays, skiing holidays are largely excuses for fake-tanned himbos called Damien to try and get off with

Taking the piste.

fake-breasted dimbettes called Helena in bars shaped like Heidi's old shed. There is a certain amount of actual skiing (see *Skiing*) but most of the time people are essentially treating the Alps as a huge, white, freezing singles bar. And with mixed results. Holiday romances are always doomed – which is good, otherwise the world would be entirely descended from waiters and drunk girls – but how much more doomed is a romance founded on *gluhwein* and fondue? Everybody likes to eat and drink on holiday, but the whole infrastructure of skiing holiday socializing is founded on what is essentially boiled Ribena and cheese soup. Not nice.

Skiing holidays are, pound for pound, the most expensive holidays in the world. From ski hire, to lift pass, to the cost of a plate of elderly crisps at 7,000 feet, you'd think you had been invited to join a sort of snow version of the Millionaire's Club. Not some daft Norwegian weirdy sport. Skiing was – and this is true – invented by Norwegians about 1,000 years ago when someone nicked their king and for some reason they could only rescue him by strapping huge lumps of bark onto their feet and sliding around like bearded penguins. After that, one might think that skiing would have been abandoned as something of a royalty-rescuing-related novelty. But the Norwegians found that a) they liked it, and b) they were good at it, so that made them one up on the Swedes and the Finns.

Then there was the last war, when being able to ski came in handy again, and the Norwegians all bought rifles and skied around the country shooting Germans. After that, they decided that there was some tourist appeal in it (skiing, that is, not shooting Germans). And now millions of people get out of perfectly nice warm beds, stumble bleary-eyed in the numbing cold past perfectly good restaurants and bars, climb up a sodding mountain on two overpriced planks – and then slide down it again. Why not cut out the middle man and just not go up the mountain in the first place?

Skiing is also a very good way of being humiliated. Having finally mastered the art of not falling over and breaking your ankles, you are just tootling down the piste when a 9-year-old girl with no ski poles races past you, firing a swathe of snow and pine cones in her wake, and causing you to fall over and break your ankles.

One of the major irritants for any skier is the *snowboarder*. Snowboarding is what the young people are into. Snowboarding is skateboarding, only with a bigger board (the great jessies) and even more silly clothing. And, as everyone knows, skateboarders are pillocks, overgrown teenagers who ought to be at work or in the army instead of clattering around an inner-city car park. In theory, snowboarders should be the same – confined to some snowy Swiss council estate that smells of frozen wee.

Nobody puts wheels on their skis and skates around on them behind Safeway, do they? So snowboards should be banned. Because a snowboard is just a skateboard with the wheels taken off, and, given that a skateboard is a plank with wheels, then a snowboard is just a plank. And there are, to coin a phrase, quite enough planks on the slopes already.

Skiers are not fond of snowboarders, and rightly so. No matter how smug and soi-disantly cool a skier may be, he or she will never be as smugbastardly self-satisfied as some tossbollock on a plank with a big

Snowboarding; note sponsor's picture on jacket.

Chalet Girls; how ugly posh kids get born.

unscary skull painted on it, whizzing along the snow like someone who washed their sled on a too-high setting.

And so to *ski resorts*. 'Resort' is pushing it. One ski-lift, one mountain and a Volvo with a broken heater does not a resort make. The better resorts have 'chalets' which suggests that they are made up of lovely, intricately carved huts, rather than old wooden Portakabins used by elks for a lavatory.

At a ski resort it is at least easy to tell the locals from the tourists. The tourists all have fantastically up-to-date and brand-new ski gear. They also have beer guts, sunburn and broken legs. The locals, in contrast, are dressed like snow tramps, and whizz around the slopes at frightening speeds.

The final irritant no skiing holiday is complete without is the *ski instructors*. They have all been skiing since they were born. They used to go to kindergarten on skis, and wear snowshoes in the house. They find skiing very easy, and are surprised that you do not. But they do not really care, because they have all become ski instructors for the same reason that Spaniards become barmen, Greeks become waiters and Germans become exchange students: to have sex with foreign women.

This is doubly easy for ski instructors because it is one of the few holiday jobs where you can guarantee that the foreign women's boyfriends will break their legs on the first day.

SURFING HOLIDAYS

Not the ones that people take in California, as those are more day trips to the beach rather than actual holidays. No, surfing holidays as we understand them in this country are very similar to camping holidays, in that they all seem to take place on a bleak cliff edge in North Devon or Cornwall. But they differ in that – simply by going on a camping holiday – you have at least achieved the purpose of the thing, which is to use up your holiday time camping. A surfing holiday is a more tragic affair. The dream is to be out every day on the waves, performing major feats of gnarly derring-do and meeting attractive young blonde women. The reality is spending

'Well, the East Coast girls are hip / I really dig the styles they wear...'

nine days trapped by a Force 6 gale in a rusting VW Camper with a Stone Roses cassette and two bottles of Zinfandel for company.

And then there's the pollution. You are more likely to catch a disease than a wave surfing in the British Isles.

If the Beach Boys had ever been forced to go on one of these surfing holidays, they would have stopped writing songs about catching a wave pretty damn sharpish and done a whole album called *Let's Go to CenterParcs Instead.*

CARAVAN HOLIDAYS

∾

There are of course two kinds of caravan holidays. One is the more familar kind, where you drag a big fridge on wheels around the country at a top speed of 17 miles an hour and try and find a field to hide it in. And the other is the really bizarre kind, where you go and stay in a caravan that has been, effectively, nailed down. The second kind is basically a more civilized sort of camping holiday (see *Camping holidays*), even if the wheelless caravans resting on bricks do look as though the bad kids from the new estate have paid them a visit in the night, and bear as much resemblance to

Good caravan.

proper camping holidays as visiting the *Cutty Sark* at Greenwich does to sailing the Atlantic single-handed.

Proper caravan holidays are among the lowest of the low, holiday-wise. This is because they revolve around one of the most useless vehicles ever invented. Once upon a time caravans were dinky things, little chalets on wheels, that a gypsy would steer through leafy English lanes in search of people who had mendable kettles. Then evolution happened, and the truly modern caravan arrived. However, unfortunately for us, it arrived in America. In America the caravan is a gorgeous beast, a section of jet fighter fuselage that piles down the highway and stops to reveal all mod cons inside, from microwave to satellite dish.

In this country, that somehow never happened. The British caravan is an evolutionary cul-de-sac, like the duck-billed platypus, or table tennis. It got so far, and then just stopped. Instead of being a gorgeous beast, etc., it is a lot of bits of tin that got together to see what the other bits of tin were doing, and then found that it was being used as a home. British caravans are huts that can move, vans with no innards, and just slightly sad things.

Outside, they advertise the past. They are either sort of rounded, like a Ford Prefect with an eating problem, or they are sharp

Bad caravan.

When stuck in holiday traffic,
why not pass the time marvelling
at the sheer variety and
hideousness of Britain's caravans?

and rectangular, like a seventies bungalow with ambitions. Inside, things are even worse. Fans of prison TV series will recognize the interior of the average caravan. A basic bunk, a low shelf, some crumbs, and primitive toilet facilities; in some ways, caravans are Strangeways on wheels. With added formica.

And this is just the caravan. Now you have got one you have to go on holiday in it. So – it's summer. You dig the caravan out of the small marsh in the garden that it has slumped into, hitch it up, and head off down the road. You get about 10 feet before hitting a traffic jam. Eventually you make it, slowly and apologetically, onto the motorway. Now the true humiliation begins, as you discover that even old ladies who are taking their late brother's car to the auctioneer's are honking at you impatiently. The anonymity of the slow lane is no refuge. You are holding up all the traffic. Worse, you're holding up all the crap traffic – the ice cream vans, the aged coaches, the Mini with ten pushbikes on the roof, and the yellow roadmendy thing. You can't go any faster and there isn't an even slower lane. Worse, there's a hill coming up.

Ten hours later, after every car in the land has honked at you, you reach your destination, a clifftop near Aberystwyth. A farmer appears and tells you to sod off. You pass the night in a lay-by. The next day you are wakened by a hammering on the door. Is it the police? No; it's a lorry driver who has confused you with the burger man's caravan.

ECO HOLIDAYS

◡

'Hi! I'm Jake. Dirta and I have been running EcoTurismo for six months now and we're delighted you've stumbled on our little website. EcoTurismo organizes ecologically friendly holidays in developing nations. That means you might pay a little more, but you'll be getting a vacation that's good for the environment as well as – we like to think! – the spirit.'

[Hi. I'm a bloke who used to have a good job in the city but I got sacked for smoking dope. My wife says she'll leave me unless I can carry on supporting her. We bought some organic marmalade once so we know what we're doing. We'll take you to a former war zone for six months and you can help the locals ruin their only crop, which is some sort of broccoli thing, walk around in mud, and maybe get bitten by an ant that carries a bowel disease. You'll sleep in a hut of your own making, and drink the local beer, which is made of the broccoli thing, and we'll charge you ten grand.]

CHRISTMAS BREAKS

◡

These are a brilliant idea. Escape from the endless torpor of relatives, party games, bad television and Britain in dead December. What could be better than getting away from all that? How about: downing a bottle of sherry in one go and sleeping behind the sofa? There is no worse time to go on holiday than Christmas. The reason is simple: everyone else who doesn't fancy the endless torpor of relatives, party games, bad television and Britain in dead December is also going on holiday. The only thing festive about a Christmas holiday is the phrase 'No room at the inn'. Had Joseph and Mary been compelled to travel via Gatwick for the Roman census, they would have found many similarities between then AD and now AD, minus the gifts from wise men, and indeed the wise men, who would have booked a cottage in Northumberland six months ago.

Everyone at the airport goes around looking like they have just

The only thing festive about a Christmas holiday is the phrase 'No room at the inn'.

heard some terrible news. They have; they have just realized that they are going on holiday with their families. They are, as Cliff Richard sang, going where the sun shines brightly. This means that they are going somewhere very far away, as the sun is currently not doing much shining brightly in the northern hemisphere. They are about to undertake an epic journey. They are taking with them Christmas presents. This makes the kids very excited, because the kids have not worked out that 'expensive Christmas holiday = rubbish Christmas presents'.

Right now, our family should be stepping out into the dazzling sunshine of a tropical airport. Instead, owing to delays caused by bad weather, they are sitting on their suitcases outside something called Sbarro trying to get some sleep. Above their heads, there is silence. There are no planes, just the gentle whoosh of Santa's sleigh as he passes overhead, on his way to some other family as they sleep in their nice warm beds.

And Santa, frankly, is the only person who should be travelling at Christmas. Everyone else should be at home, gearing up for the most boring day of the year. Just because the Queen pre-records her Christmas broadcast so she can shove off to Scotland for the season doesn't mean that we can do the same. Shove off to Scotland, that is, not pre-record our Christmas broadcasts.

Oh, and don't take any Christmas crackers with you, because they'll be confiscated at the airport as 'weapons'. Blimey, the jokes aren't that bad.

PACKAGE HOLIDAYS
∾

Many years ago the Mediterranean was ringed with tiny fishing villages, each one indistinguishable from the other with their toothless old locals, boats with eyes painted on them, nets drying on

Nowadays reps are more like youth TV presenters who fell into the amphetamine cauldron when they were babies.

the beach, and Sophia Loren lookalikes wondering why no film producers ever came by for the shrimp harvest. The seasons trickled away slowly in these villages, and it would have been hard for any passing time travellers to work out what year it was, technology being largely confined to a huge radio in the local bar and the sophisticated radar equipment in the village smuggling fleet.

Then the 1960s happened, and package holidays were invented. This meant that now travellers could book their entire holiday as an, as it were, package. No more did we need to write to the Hotel Splendide enquiring about rooms months in advance, book passage on the *SS Lactose-Intolerant* and then reserve a compartment on the Mauve Train. Now we could just go into a travel agent (see *Travel agents*) and do the whole lot in one go. Bliss was it to be young and going on a package holiday in that dawn. Until, of course, you got there.

Anybody who has ever endured a 1970s' sitcom will be familiar with the 'holiday episode' when the entire cast take a package holiday to some resort called, as a rule, the Costa Packet. Here the same story always unfolded, comfortable like a folk tale – the unbuilt rooms ('It's a five-star hotel!' 'Yes, I can see four of them through the hole in the ceiling!'), the debris-filled swimming pools, the filthy food, the foreign booze… In short, the ideal holiday for the 1970s' British tourist. Raised in a culture of whingeing and complaining, where the highest praise – 'Mustn't grumble' – implied that grumbling was man's natural state, Brits on holiday could not possibly be happy unless they had something to moan about. And a budget holiday in a Fascist state where they couldn't make a decent cup of tea was it. After that, the floodgates were open.

One important element of the package holiday that is regrettably still part of the package is the *holiday rep*. There was a time when a holiday rep was a clean-cut, ironed-trousered chap or girl with a

That same day, doctors removed the microphone surgically.

broad smile, a firm handshake and a list of table-tennis-related activities. They were like redcoats without the exhibitionism (see *Redcoats and Bluecoats*), and they were there for a good reason: to ensure that the jet-lagged, half-awake British tourists who had never been south of Southend before would actually make it to their hotels and, once at the hotel, would not wander off into the jungle or village and be eaten by tigers, or fishermen. At the end of the holiday they would gather all the tourists together and make sure they got on the plane home again. Reps were, in short, reliable, useful people.

Nowadays reps are more like youth TV presenters who fell into the amphetamine cauldron when they were babies. They still meet you at the airport, but instead of a clipboard they will have a baseball cap with a plastic dog turd on the brim. They will have names like Bazzer, Donkey and Meltdown, and there will be no mention of table tennis unless it involves nudity or lager.

Bazzer, Donkey and Meltdown will take you to the hotel on the minibus ('This is your driver, Miguel. We call him Mister Tinywinkle.'), but instead of taking down your names they will take down their trousers. Instead of a thorough explanation of local customs, there will be a drinking game on the bus. As you cringe at the back, hoping that you will not be noticed, you realize that you are, in fact, in hell.

The rest of the holiday will be ruined in a similar manner by these freaks. Every night there will be an increasingly unpleasant activity to endure. Maybe it will be a karaoke night that is somehow themed to the movies of Quentin Tarantino. Perhaps there will be a drinking game which involves humiliating the more obese members of your party. Either way, it will be slightly less pleasant than being whipped through the streets at noon by gorillas.

Once upon a time people had never been to any foreign countries, except to invade them, and there was a whole world out there prepared to serve you chips and paella.

The only consolation of such a vacation is that your torturers are only putting you through this mill of damnation because – astonishingly – they want to be liked. The fact that nobody has ever been liked because they made a shy teenager drink a bucket of cigarette ends does not occur to them. Deep down, the reps want to be friends with you. Unfortunately they cannot interact with other people in a normal way, so they have to torture them. (The Spanish Inquisition probably started out the same way, with Torquemada noticing that the other priests seemed to be having more of a good time than him.)

We know that the reps want to be liked because, unlike Torquemada, they are democratic in their vileness. They inflict the same punishments on themselves too. So as you are forced to do the Birdie Song in a uniform that Prince Harry might favour, minus the shorts, you can console yourself with the knowledge that later on Bazzer, Donkey or Meltdown will be bobbing for catfood in a barrel of wee, and, much later on, crying themselves to sleep in a bed whose sheets have been drenched in cider and scorpions.

18–30 HOLIDAYS

∾

If you want constant bad sex with spotty alcoholics, more cheap booze than even a Dean Martin the size of Cuba could handle, all-night dancing to the worst music ever recorded, and a blank white cube to sleep in that smells of your own vomit you are:

a in need of psychiatric care;
b in need of a condom for your liver;
c on an 18–30 holiday.

Or indeed all three. As much a product of the vile 1980s as Thatcherism, Simple Minds and puffball skirts, the 18–30 holiday was in fact the logical end-product of the original package holidays of the 1960s. Once upon a time these were liberating things, a chance for young ignorant Brits to see a foreign country and impose their own culture on it. People had never been to any foreign countries,

*Despair and bodily fluids
combine for the perfect
Ibiza night out.*

except to invade them, and
there was a whole world out
there prepared to serve you
chips and paella. But soon it
was not enough to drink
Double Diamond and take
our trousers off during 'Y
Viva Espana'. People wanted
more. They wanted a holiday
that explicitly promised
sexual intercourse. Drunken,
sunburned, oafish sexual
intercourse, with people who
had travelled abroad specifically to have that drunken, sunburned,
oafish sexual intercourse, so you were actually in with a chance. The
fact that most people on 18–30 holidays still failed to get their ends
away despite being surrounded by beer-sodden would-be shaggers
suggests either that for some people lakes of alcohol still aren't enough
to act as an ugly filter, or that in the end their ideal would be to get
off with a crate of Hofmeister.

The other frightening thing about the 18–30 holiday is the word
'30'. At the 18 end it's understandable that teenagers want to not so
much lose their virginity as deny ever having met it. At the 30 end
something unsavoury begins to creep in. And that something has a
beer belly, a small house in the Midlands and no girlfriend. Like Dirk
Bogarde's character in *Death in Venice*, only wearing a knock-off
Hackett rugby shirt with a curry stain over the navel, he is in search of
love for the last time before sinking slowly in the west. Unlike Dirk
Bogarde's character, he is not looking for a idealized soulmate, just
someone who will admire his vocabulary of catchphrases from defunct
sketch shows, and sleep with him when they are drunk. Nobody does,

so he will end up being thrown out of a minicab two nights later, a minicab being the only place he can get into after nine pints.

No doubt this is not what the organizers of these fine holidays ever had in mind. No, they were probably hoping for something classier (see *Holidays that end up on cable TV*).

HOLIDAYS THAT END UP ON CABLE TV

∿

These days an 18–30 holiday is not enough. Ever since the inhabitants of tiny islands with no plumbing were discovered by rave fans who needed no plumbing because they were going to stay up all night, mere debauchery is just the tip of the shagberg. In the 1980s people started to go to far-off locations like Ayia Napa, Ibiza and Goa because they could dance all night and when in the morning they collapsed on the beach in an inchoate state they wouldn't freeze to death. In fact, when they woke up it would be nice and sunny, and they could buy some beads or an ice cream. All in all, much pleasanter than waking up in Scarborough with a donkey licking their eyelids off.

Raves began as sort of culty, exclusive things far away from home that only nine DJs knew about. But after a while the DJs got fed up of just going to each other's raves and feeling jealous, so they let other people come. Soon the tiny islands were full of people who did not care who the DJs were, so long as there was beer and drugs to buy. They danced and drank and had it off in the streets, while the locals sold them beer and fags and then ran away.

After a while these holidays became so popular that even TV companies got to hear about them. With many empty hours to fill, and no money to pay anyone, the TV companies were ecstatic at the thought of people who would have drunken sex in exotic locations in front of the cameras, for free. Soon our screens were filled, not with the quality drama that we had expected from today's marvellous TV companies, but with men and women lifting their tops to reveal huge wobbling sun-reddened breasts. A visitor from another world

Boy! Wait till they find out where bad girls really go!

would have gained the impression that these places were inhabited by headless tits. And in a way, they would have been right.

The ravers, embarrassed, moved on to trendier locations to find the nine DJs. The drunks and the sex-seekers continue to arrive, but these days they won't get drunk or have sex in front of a camera unless they get paid first. So very soon these tiny islands will bear witness to the sight of TV crews getting drunk and having sex in front of each other, just to fill up the empty hours. Serve 'em right, too.

SPACE HOLIDAYS

～

Well, all right, not actually going to the Moon or Mars or anything like that, but it is possible to book short flights into space now, if you go to the former Soviet Union, or 'McDonald's' as it is now known. The great technology that sent the heroes of our youth into space – Yuri Gagarin and Laika the space dog being but two – is now being used to boost millionaire tourists into orbit. Once the sky was full of cosmonauts (and space dogs) threatening the very fabric of capitalism. Now it is full of millionaires being strapped into bits of old Soyuz capsules. It is a sad decline for the might of the Soviet space programme, but there is a bit of consolation. Some conspiracy theorists believe that the Russians are not just sending big fat rich Westerners into Earth's orbit, they are also leaving them up there. This may or may not be true; certainly, if Richard Branson ever fancies a trip into space, we can but hope.

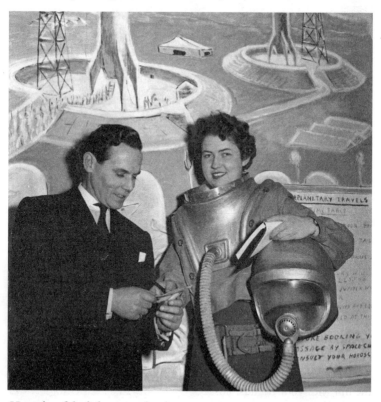

How they faked the moon landings.

'DANGEROUS HOLIDAYS'

∾

All holidays are dangerous in some way, especially if boredom can be counted as a danger. But there is another kind of dangerous holiday, undertaken by people who want 'thrills' in their lives, people who feel the need for 'the adrenaline rush', so they pack up their oddly gayesque army surplus travel wear – including those pointless padded waistcoats with tiny pockets suitable only for transporting My Little Pony figurines – buy a very manly knife that gets confiscated at Luton Airport, and head out to some poor beleaguered land where people are being killed for their beliefs, and have a holiday. Then they come back and bang on about how 'close to the edge' they were, when the local rebel militia just couldn't be bothered to waste the bullets.

A week in Provence is a lot more appealing than a whole year in Provence.

HOLIDAYS IN PLACES WHERE BOOKS AND FILMS HAVE BEEN SET

∾

Always an error. Anybody who has spent two weeks in a damp boarding house in Haworth because they were attracted by the romance of the Brontës can confirm this. Similarly, any fool who saw the *Lord of the Rings* films and goes to New Zealand because they might see an orc is clearly equally deluded.

However, there is a happy flipside to this. Visiting places where appalling films have been made has two advantages. One, there are few people visiting that place where they filmed *Captain Corelli's Mandolin* because it wasn't very good. And two, it is very nice there. Of course, if you go to Holmfirth, where they keep filming *Last of the Summer Wine*, a tin bath on wheels is provided so you can roll down the hill with your friends. Possibly. And, equally of course, a week in Provence is a lot more appealing than a whole year in Provence.

Thousands flock to the place where they film 'Last of the Summer Wine'. Well, it's better than watching it on telly.

On the other hand, if you take a trip to the Tunisian desert because that's where they filmed the latest *Star Wars* movies, you deserve everything you get. Everything.

HOLIDAY CAMPS
~

For you the war is over, Tommy. There has always been an uncanny, and much-mentioned, similarity between the great British holiday camp and the prison camps of the Second World War. Admittedly, nobody was ever shot for trying to get out of Pontin's, but then nobody at Colditz was ever forced to enter a Knobbly Knees contest. Holiday camps, like pleurisy, were once everywhere, but both now are mercifully rare. This is because of two major factors. One was the discovery, perhaps late in Britain, of other, pleasanter lands where holidays could be taken without being

In the olden days a holiday camp was the sort of place where you would be forced out of bed at 5 a.m. by sirens to go and eat a breakfast that was not so much hearty as heart-attacky.

drowned in torrents of rain or surfeited with chips in brown gravy. The other was the gradual absorption of all the little holiday camps – the Potters, the Mugleys, the Jempsons, or whatever long-gone names these places had – into two great empires. These empires exist today: Butlins, founded by Billy Butlin, and Pontins, presided over by Fred Pontin. Billy is commemorated now by the 'popular' Butlins mascot, Billy Bear, a bear that apparently wants to become a Redcoat (see *Redcoats and Bluecoats*). Fred is remembered by many people of a certain age for his appearances in the Pontins telly ads, where he would sit silently in the background as a lackey reeled off the many joys of a Pontins holiday. At the end of the advert the lackey would turn to his master, and this was Fred's signal to raise his thumb in the air and declare, with all the wobbly dignity of Young Mister Grace, 'Book early!'

Sadly, Fred and Billy are gone, but their dream lives on. However, now it's a loud, brightly coloured, slightly unpleasant sort of dream. Holiday camps have changed a lot over the years. In the olden days they were the sort of place where you would be forced out of bed at 5 a.m. by sirens to go and eat a breakfast that was not so much hearty as heart-attacky. You would then spend the day engaged in regimented fun, until evening came when you would be sent back to your chalet to sleep. At which point you would wait until the guards were asleep, then get up and build a glider.

Now, of course, holiday camps are entirely different. Here is a quick multiple-choice questionnaire about today's modern holiday camps, based on real claims in actual holiday camp literature. Pick the response that most suits your viewpoint.

1   'Bob the Builder is coming to Butlins!'
a   Hurrah! Fun for all the family.
b   Oh, Christ.

2   'Whether you're into Motown Legends, Brass Bands or Country Music, you'll find the sounds you like.'
a   At last, a chance to see a lot of groups where all the famous members left years ago.
b   Oh, Christ.

3   'If it's action and entertainment you're after, look no further than Pontin's Camber Sands Centre.'
a   Might be a bit too exciting. Have they got Crazy Golf?
b   Oh, Christ.

4   'Buckleys Yesterday's World – voted Top Attraction in the South East 2002. Visit the Victorian kitchen, 1930s wireless shop, pharmacy, 1960s television store, country railway station and much more.'
a   There's more? Like a 1920s hunger march? Or a 1914–18 war?
b   Oh, Christ.

5   Puppet Castle – New adventures with Billy Bear – Billy in The Haunted House at Bognor Regis, Billy and the Pirate Treasure at Minehead and Billy's Magic Toy Shop at Skegness.
a   Looks like Billy's got this town sewn up.
b   Oh, Ch—! A Puppet Castle? Cool!

How did you do?
Mostly 'a's: You are a born optimist. Holiday camps are for you. Book early!

Mostly 'b's: You are a cynical sod for whom fun is an alien world. But you knew that already.

REDCOATS AND BLUECOATS

~

As holiday reps are to package holidays, so Redcoats and Bluecoats are to holiday camps. Billy Butlin had his Redcoats. Fred Pontin, for whom an idea wasn't an idea unless Billy Butlin had road-tested it, had his Bluecoats. Whether or not Redcoats and Bluecoats used to meet in big fields and engage in open combat is not recorded, but it would have been a fine sight, like great battles of the American Revolution re-enacted in blazers. Many great entertainers and Shane Ritchie began their careers as Bluecoats, while the Redcoats have owned up to Cilla Black, Des O'Connor and Cliff Richard. For both Red and Blue, the results were the same. You turned up to some godforsaken concrete outdoor bunker, performed a collection of nightmarish vaudeville routines and, having got the job, were licensed to upset and annoy decent working folk in their free time. This was, quite rightly, considered excellent preparation for a career in light entertainment, where you got to do all the same things all over again, only in black and white.

Nowadays any budding Shane Ritchie who wishes to share their outgoing personality with a wider audience goes in for TV talent contests where they are judged by people even smugger than they are.

MURDER MYSTERY WEEKENDS

~

These are bizarre events. There is in theory nothing wrong with getting tanked up and claiming to be Paige Turner, the celebrated novelist, or Ava Cigar, the vampish Hollywood starlet, and then accusing a stranger of murder. It can be quite dramatic, and is a great excuse for suddenly shouting, 'YOU MURDERING BASTARD!' at somebody you don't like. (Warning: Do not try this in the pub.)

Redcoats wear these sunglasses to stop eagles diving down and plucking out their stupid eyes.

But a murder mystery weekend? No thank you. A whole two or three days in some awful country hovel that forgot to take its two AA stars down after they found a mouse in the soufflé is no fun at all. Spending a whole sodding weekend dressed as Alec Smart, the society gossip, or Noel Plates, the racing driver, and having to talk to a lot of people in flaming character might appeal to a simpleton or an unemployed actor, but anyone else's reaction must involve flight.

There are a couple of ways out of this egregious time-warped hellhole. You can take over – shouting normally does it – and suggest that we drop the boring old country house theme and do Drive-By Crack Dealer Execution murder mystery weekends instead, so at least you get to go out a bit. Or how about a Murder by Boring Murder Mystery Weekend mystery weekend, where tedium is your weapon as you get to devise your own specially annoying and complicated murder mystery.

If all else fails, just play along, await your opportunity, stand up suddenly and say, 'My name is Major Pollux the disgraced ex-Guards officer, and I am the murderer. Yes, I did it. Now let me take off this ridiculous dinner jacket and go home.' Never fails.

HOLIDAY COTTAGES 1
~

Older readers, see *Wales*.

HOLIDAY COTTAGES 2
~

When one has reached a certain age, one tires of crowded holiday resorts and jammed-up beaches, and longs for a quiet seaside or moorland cottage to spend the holidays in. Unfortunately, unless one has married, or is a Beckham, one has to go and rent the bugger. And thus was born the holiday cottage trade.

Holiday cottages are all the same. They look like something from the novels of Enid Blyton in the brochure, except you can drink whisky in them. They seem quite cheap, really, and not too hard to get to. Once booked, however – and here 'booking' is a word

Holiday cottages look like something from the novels of Enid Blyton in the brochure, except you can drink whisky in them.

that means 'piling on hidden charges until your wallet cries' – the cottage changes. It is no longer not too hard to get to. It is in fact at the far end of a road that itself goes through a field and some bogs, after taking on the duties of a path

that doubles as a ponies' toilet. It is not on the map you printed out, or in the *AA Book of Remote Muddy Destinations*. In fact, you will only find the cottage by complete accident, after uttering the magic words, 'Of course I don't know where we are. Do I look like I know where we are?'

By now it is 4 o'clock in the morning, and you have used up about nine hours of your pathetically short holiday weekend actually driving. You stagger out of the car, through at least four kinds of dark soft matter, and search for the key. You are doing this alone as your map-reader is now using the map to find the nearest pub. The key is not 'under the mat' unless 'mat' is a country phrase meaning 'with the people at the next farm'. You decide to break in, which is not hard as the front door isn't locked.

Turning on the lights, you are indeed greeted with a sight from an Enid Blyton novel, but it is not the rose-walled cottage that the four young sleuths are staying in, it is the dungeon that Jim-Jim the smuggler imprisons them in. The air is damp, the walls are damp, even the furniture is damp. You slump on a sofa that appears to have spent most of its career as a bed for very old Labradors, and count to fifty before going to get the luggage. Then you fall asleep on the sofa.

In the morning you awake to find that the cottage has been transformed. Light pours in. Bees buzz outside and flowers release their morning scents. As do the drains, which are full of vintage leaves and a dead bat. There is also something chittering in the chimney-breast. Nature is here, as evinced by the mouse droppings in the bread-bin and the *Guinness Book of Records*-sized colony of silverfish in the knife drawer.

You explore the cottage, taking note of the mattresses, which appear to have been first soaked in beer and then had cannonballs dropped on them, judging by the dents. The walls are so cracked they look like the Koran in the original Arabic, and the ceiling is supported by bowing beams and a forest of spider's webs. Wiping the dead flies from the windows, you look out at the view; a gorgeous rustic slaughterhouse to the west, and a concrete sty full of enormous pigs to the east.

Running downstairs, you put your foot through a step. You stagger into the front room, taking time to observe a complete set of Enid Blyton novels on the shelf where a TV has never been, and collapse once more on the sofa.

Only six and a half days to go…

HERITAGE PROPERTIES
∾

Very in, these days. Heritage properties are buildings of historical interest, like castles, follies and small manor houses, that can now be rented by scruffy members of the grubby public for holidays, so long as they don't put coal in the bath or hoist ponies into the attic on a home-made winch. These properties always look nice in the hand-tooled brochure, where they have been photographed from a helicopter or represented in the form of eighteenth-century paintings. In reality they have at least one of the following problems: they are freezing, they are miles from anywhere, and/or they are tiny. We know that people were smaller in the old days, but some of these places are taking the mickey. Sindy and Action Man would have a hard time spending the weekend in one of them.

The financial aspect is equally disconcerting. You are told in the brochure how much money the company has spent restoring the property to its former glory. This must be your fault in some way, as you are apparently paying for the restoration single-handed. And as for 'former glory', it seems unlikely that the original architect's intent was to install little fringey lamps, a musty-smelling mini-fridge, and a TV that claims to get five channels but only gets three, two of them twice.

LAS VEGAS VACATIONS
∿

Calling a trip to Las Vegas a city break is a bit like calling the Battle of Jericho a visit from some Jehovah's Witnesses. Unlike other cities, Las Vegas only exists as a place to visit. True, it has inhabitants, and houses to put them in, but these people are there almost by coincidence, or as extras to fill in the gaps between casinos. Las Vegas is, we are told, a theme park. This blindingly obvious remark explains everything about the town, whose name means 'Where's my wallet?' in English. It explains why Las Vegas is full of model versions of famous buildings from many lands. Vegas has just edited down the world to the bits tourists are interested in – the Eiffel Tower, the Empire State Building, the Seattle Space Needle – and left out all the other stuff. Cynics may say this is just an accurate map of the world from an American point of view that only needs Araby Land to complete it, but everyone else just thinks how much nicer the models are and how much easier to visit compared to the larger, grubbier originals (see *Landmarks and wonders*).

A LONDON WEEKEND
∿

There's something very weird about spending your holiday in a town. True, it's a short break, otherwise it would be so expensive that you'd be better off actually renting a flat. True, you don't have to worry about self-catering and so on, because the hotel lays on a regular supply of second-rate meals, only two of which aren't already included in the bill (the third one, lunch, isn't included in the bill because they don't do it). And true, your room does have all the conveniences of home, if your home is one where the kettle and the

Madame Tussauds; full of bloody foreigners as usual.

iron used to belong to a pixie and the bathroom has a phone in it in case you need to phone someone up and say, 'Hi! I'm in the bathroom!' But otherwise, city breaks are bloody strange.

For a start, you're on holiday in a hotel in a big city, but you're not abroad. This means that what is exotic and fun in a foreign country – that is, local manners and customs – is less so in your homeland. For example, the cab driver who charges you double would, abroad, be a charming local rogue. In Britain he is a thieving swine. The meal you had in the restaurant around the corner would, elsewhere, be a lesson in the differences between our two cuisines. In Britain it's a plate of monkey swill that you are not paying forty quid for. And the TV film channel in the hotel room that in Europe might be an amusing parade of cheap regional quirkiness or actual hardcore porn is in Britain a load of five-year-old crap movies that you've seen on telly six times already.

Still, you can always hit the town. Here are some of the delightful things you can do:

1 Go on a walking tour. This means that you will have to meet a
man dressed as Sherlock Holmes or Sergeant Pepper who will
guide you and six Japanese men around town, pointing out
things that often have only a vague connection to the tour's
theme. Over there is a shed on the site of a theatre where the
Beatles once had their photograph taken. Over here is a street
sign that replaced the one under which Dr Watson was clubbed
to the ground, or would have been had he existed. This shop is
next door to where a tube station used to be. After an hour of
the tour you start to think he is making it up. How does he
know that Lenin drank in Dunkin' Donuts? Was there really an
underground river on the second floor of Debenhams?

2 Go to a show. You are the only person who hates it. This is
because you have suppressed the child inside you. You have
failed to follow your dreams. You are a shameful person.
Fortunately you don't care because you lined up six vodkas in
the interval and now you are asleep, much to the annoyance
of the party from Dusseldorf behind you.

3 Go into the red light district. Be sure to be slightly drunk and

The frighteningness of this scene is only outweighed by the authenticity.

wearing a football shirt, so that the bouncers know to let you in
and the bar staff know to charge you £500 for a bottle of
Pommery.

4 Go clubbing in a superclub. This is the only way you can
exactly reproduce all the fun of being on a ferry on dry land
(see *Ferries*). Do not try to buy duty-free goods, though.

5 Go shopping. As you are in Britain, the huge store you are
shopping in is exactly the same as the one where you live,
except with more shirts and much higher prices.

6 Go to the cinema, and see a film four days before it opens in
your home town, for about twice the price.

7 Visit an exhibition. Pretend that the fire extinguishers are part
of the show! Praise the canteen staff for the dryness of their
food! Buy a postcard of an exhibit that you didn't see!

8 Get to the station early. It has the same shops, restaurants and
facilities as the rest of the city you are in, and it's cheaper, too.

9 Want to visit a gay disco and go for a country walk but
don't have time to do both? Visit Hampstead Heath and take
a Walkman.

10 Drop some books to hear the echo in the British Museum
Reading Room. First editions fall hardest.

THE 10 MOST POPULAR HOLIDAY DESTINATIONS

Short haul

1 *Balearic Islands*. The Spanish have very sensibly established
Britain's favourite holiday destination as far away from their
mainland as possible. This is to ensure that as few actual
Spanish people as possible have to meet any of the beer-crazed,
pie-eating, Union-Jack-faced lard gimps who go there.

2 *Greece*. Their soldiers dress like the ghosts of effeminate
Scotsmen, all pompoms and kilts. The best things in their
country are in ruins. It's too hot. They drink engine oil instead of

wine. No wonder they were so bored that they were forced to invent democracy.

3   *Mainland Spain*. Some Brits get through to the Spanish mainland. There they find a lot of flat plains, some paella, and the least convincing Flamenco dancing outside the Midlands. So they go back to the Balearics again.

4   *Turkey*. Like Greece, only without the ruins and the effeminate military, Turkey has the edge for Brits as regards a shared culinary language – 'doner', 'kebab' and 'shish' will keep you going.

5   *Canary Islands*. Named because of the yellow songbirds found there. However, a better name might be The Beer-Crazed Pie-eating Union-Jack-Faced Lard Gimp Islands.

Long haul

1   *Florida*. It used to be all bogs and alligators, but now it has been drained to make way for old Americans and Mickey Mouse. Nostalgia for the old Florida runs high.

2   *Mexico*. 'Badges? We don't need no stinking badges!' Or efficient car rental firms, or completed swimming pools, or people who shave. The 1970s Spain of the twenty-first century.

3   *Dominican Republic*. It is a surprise to the travel-minded to see a small Central American nation so high on this list. It is less of a surprise to note that people do not go to the Dominican Republic to explore its unique culture. They go because the beaches and the hotels are exactly like those in Benidorm and Torremolinos.

4   *Margarita*. A resort named after a drink? Of course British people will go there. See also Beer in Devon, Champagne in France and Snakebite in Queensland.

5   *Jamaica*. It is hard to think well of this so-called 'relaxing' and 'chilled-out' holiday destination when you are listening to your fourteenth bad Bob Marley song of the day played by a busker who will only stop playing when he falls over, overwhelmed by his own skunk fumes.

GETTING THERE

PACKING

'Left it till the last minute as usual.' People often tut and say this to you as if you are some fly-by-night nincompoop. Perhaps they think you should have a suitcase ready and packed all the time – a good idea if you want to take a heap of ageing, crumpled clothes on holiday with you, as well as the best novels of 1987 and some toothpaste that has burned its way out into the world through its own tube. Fashions change, even yours. If you leave it to the last minute you may forget the odd scarf or razor, but at least you won't be

Woman in front of you in airport check-in, 1959.

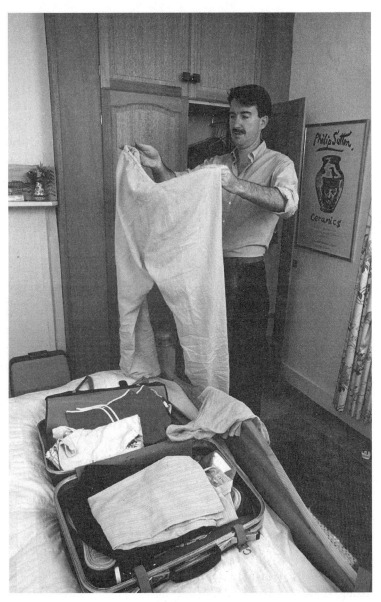

'Hmmm... do I really need TWO pairs of giant gay pants?'

going round on holiday looking like an extra in *The Breakfast Club*.

Then there is the vexed issue of clothing. Does it ever rain in Torremolinos? (Yes, the whole time you will be there.) Is it ever hot and sunny on an Alpine ski holiday? (Yes again.) What about the Gobi desert? (As changeable as a maiden's heart. Take galoshes, sweaters, swimming trunks, sandals and hiking boots.)

This is why many people end up taking hundreds of suitcases full of clothing, most of which they won't wear. The simpler option is to pack no clothes, take all your savings, and buy clothing when you get out there.

LEAVING THE HOUSE 1:
THE PAPERS AND THE MILK
∼

Cancel them? And let the milkman and the newsagent – gossips both and with criminal records, possibly – know that you'll be away? No thanks. The security of your home is worth a few pints of cheese on the doorstep. Besides, what greater satisfaction can there be than coming home to a fortnight's worth of out-of-date newspapers and seeing for yourself that you have failed to miss any important events?

And if you come home to find you've been burgled and Britain has accidentally voted in a government of cannibals, you can live off the cheese.

LEAVING THE HOUSE 2:
GIVING THE KEYS TO THE NEIGHBOURS
∼

Why not just give them the house? Giving the keys to the neighbours is not only a physical act, it's a symbolic one. Now they are your friends. Let them watch over your home while you're away and you'll be saying a tacit 'OK' to their loud music, motorbike-fixing, smoky bonfires and swingers' parties. Plus when you're away they'll be using your house for their swingers' parties.

No, save time and effort. Get some red paint and write the word PLAGUE on your front door just before you leave. You never know, it might work.

LEAVING THE HOUSE 3: TIMERS

~

Some people recommend the use of timers to fool burglars. They say that setting your lights, TV and so forth to come on at various times will trick burglars into thinking you're at home. No, it won't. Why? Because any burglar watching your house will observe your apparently astonishingly regular habits, deduce that when you go to bed you really go to bed, wait till the lights go out, and then burgle you. And, on finding the house unoccupied, will became enraged and do that thing with the toothbrush and the Polaroid camera.

> **For a document that, in your case, is at least as important as the Magna Carta, the passport is surprisingly loseable.**

PASSPORT 1

~

A dreadful invention. For a start, what the hell does the Home Secretary think he's doing, guaranteeing your safety and affording you protection wherever you go? Nobody wants to be having a quiet cocktail in Miami when all of a sudden a Cabinet Minister hoves into view, warning you about the dangers of hard liquor. It's all lies, anyway; as everyone who's ever been stuck at Heathrow with the delayed flight of all delayed flights knows, there is little or no chance of the Home Secretary doing anything about it. The Defence Secretary would be a much better person to be doing the protecting; with at least three armed forces at his disposal, he could have you in Knossos by teatime. And get some proper biscuits to go with your tea.

PASSPORT 2

◠

Where is it? For a document that, in your case, is at least as important as the Magna Carta, the passport is surprisingly loseable. To ensure you can find it without turning the house upside

down, passports ought to be at least 10 feet long, luminous orange, and with a weep-weep alarm like a car that you can activate from several miles away. But they're not; they're just big postage stamps, really. With a really bad photograph of you after your kidneys failed and you were punched in the face in a pub by accident.

And while we're on the subject, why does it say in the back, 'This passport contains 32 (numbered) pages'? In eleven different languages? Is this for the benefit of Finnish customs officials who've never seen numbers before? Makes you want to rip a page out and write 'No it doesn't' beside it.

It's in the drawer with the holiday snaps, by the way.

This man is under royal protection.

LEAVING THE HOUSE 4

◠

Then there's doubt. What doubt does is assail people. When doubt assails you is, generally speaking, almost at once. Have you left the gas on? Have you cancelled the milk? Have you turned the dangerously primitive central heating system off? Did you leave one, or possibly all, of the windows open? Did the new neighbours who closely resemble a family of Victorian footpads see you leave the house, obviously to go away for a fortnight?

Of course, doubt can easily be assuaged by going back home and checking all these things. But as you are late you can't do this, so you spend the entire holiday in a frenzy of worry and angst.

LEAVING THE HOUSE 5

Of course, all the things you genuinely did forget to do will not occur to you until it's almost too late, or altogether too late. One of the things you have forgotten will almost certainly be your cargo, human or otherwise, and you'll have to go back and get it. There is a law of physics which states that, the more indispensable the item, the nearer to your destination you will be when someone notices it is missing. Thus:

Item	Discovered missing when
Toothbrush	Locking the house up
Child's teddy bear	On the motorway
Tickets	At the check-in desk
Child	Watching *Home Alone* on the plane

KENNELS

Pets: Can't take 'em with you, can't leave 'em in the house to work things out for themselves. Owing to their various genuine animal problems (apparent incontinence, belief that furniture is food) and their imagined human-like problems (they will miss Male Feeding Machine and Female Feeding Machine), animals cannot be left to look after the house when their owners are on holiday. They are, despite their inflated reputation as guards and things people should beware of, rubbish at looking after the house. At least dogs bark; cats do nothing and would, if given the chance, let any burglars in just for the hell of it. There are no tasks that a pet can do. The hoovering will remain

Animals are, despite their inflated reputation as guards, rubbish at looking after the house. The hoovering will remain undone.

undone, the dishes left in the sink, and your pets would sooner bark at a ringing telephone than actually trouble themselves to pick it up.

And you can't take them with you. True, you can get a passport for your pet these days, but the thought of having to lug the hound across Europe for weeks is somewhat depressing. Dogs are homey creatures and international walkies will not suit them. Plus getting a cat into a photo booth for its pet passport photo sounds like something even the bravest of us might wish to avoid. Oh, and they might get bitten by some foreign animals and give you rabies. Being able to froth at the mouth at will could be useful at a meeting with your bank to complain about your overdraft, but is generally inadvisable.

So the only solution is to put the pets in kennels or a cattery. (NB.

In modern kennels, pets have plenty to do and are rarely bored.

No matter how tempted you are to disguise your dog as a cat or vice versa, it is a bad idea to put your pet in the wrong place. But a fun one.) This is ridiculous but necessary. Paying a bunch of over-enthusiastic and frankly animal-smelling teenagers to feed your pets when they would be happy with some sort of carcass in the back yard – the pets, not the teenagers – is a ludicrous expense. Taking them for walks is equally nuts. But it is probably illegal to tie all the pets to a big pole in the middle of an exercise yard and make sudden noises so they all run around and get tired.

Kennels it is then, and a huge bill when you get home. (See *Huge bill when you get home*.)

PLANTS

❧

These are like animals, only quieter, and therefore more likely to fade away while you are on your hols. Nobody knows how to care for plants while on holiday. You can't put them in kennels, a basset hound might dig them up. You can put them in the bath, remembering first to add some water. This will at best upset any burglars, who will think that some sort of plant man is having a bath when they break in, and at worst leave a mulching, rotting heap of dead matter in your bath that will honk of compost for months after you come home.

Or you can 'trust' the neighbours to water them. Just try to avoiding telling Mr Harris next door, 'Give them as much water as you put in a glass of whisky – and as often.'

DRIVING TO THE AIRPORT / FERRY PORT / RAILWAY STATION

❧

There are no unfraught journeys on a holiday. Even spending the weekend in the attic or up a tree would involve some sort of hellish trip or other. But actually going from your nice, safe, immobile home to a holiday jumping-off point is beyond horrific.

Driving to the airport is not the time to try that new short cut. But you will.

Directional problems

You will get lost. Possibly at the end of the very street where you live. Failing that, your map-reader will skip six pages and send you towards Irkutsk. You could get one of those Global Satellite Positioning things where a map comes up and you have to drive along it like a computer game car, herded along by a clinical German woman saying 'Turn left' every five seconds. To be avoided unless, that is, you enjoy looking at a tiny little map while being told what to do by a German robot and trying to drive a car at the same time, so you end up in a pond, or the middle of Tesco's.

Traffic

Now is not the time to try that new short cut. But you will. And so will hundreds of other people. This also has the knock-on effect of completely emptying the overcrowded motorway you normally use. As you spend another hour in a too-warm car in the middle of several thousand other cars, your egg and cress sandwiches on the turn, your 4 year old being violently unwell into a magazine on the back seat, and the nearest loo in a different county, now is not a good time for your passengers to suggest that you should have gone 'the normal way'. But they will.

Queues possible

In-car entertainment

On your own, you might play Radio Four, or perhaps some long-forgotten raucous album of your youth. With the kids in the car, everything goes to hell. Basically, it's

Left: They could only get three cars on the sign.

going to be a drive of several hundred miles listening to a loop tape of 'The Wheels on the Bus (Go Round and Round)'.

Breakdown

There is a slight chance that your car will break down. How slight a chance? About as slight a chance as rain in the Midlands or an outbreak of bad manners in Paris. There is no way you can prepare for this event, short of marrying an AA man. (NB. This does not always work.)

Breaking down in a foreign country is even worse. To get back on the road again will involve hundreds of pounds, a huge mobile phone bill, an actual real-life walk up a long windy road with an actual petrol can like in a cartoon, a conversation with a mechanic whose head was the model for Super Mario, and finally your car will be replaced for some reason with a rusty Seat so small that it may well have been garaged in a Christmas cracker.

COACHES

∾

Those of us who opt for coach travel do so for many reasons. None of these reasons will ever be 'because coaches are nice'. Coaches are very much not nice. They are, essentially, sheds that have got loose and been allowed to crawl up and down motorways like metal snails. Coaches combine the worst aspects of trains and planes – cramped, uncomfortable, dull – with a few of their own. You will always end up in a window seat, which sounds nice, except the window somehow looks out only onto the M25 and completely fogs up after twenty minutes. After you are settled in, the fattest man in the world will sit next to you and, five seconds before you realize you need to get up, will fall asleep, in an unwakeable manner, and snore like a huge statue being dragged over gravel all the way to Honiton.

All this is assuming you have a coach driver who isn't wearing his wife's reading glasses, or has sobered up, or isn't scared of flashing lights, or doesn't have a mobile in one hand and a child perched like a living mascot on the dashboard.

Blast! Two weeks driving around Europe and I forgot to get out of the coach!

FERRIES

Once upon a time you knew where you were with ferries. They were large, cold things that smelled of seasickness and beer, like a huge boatswain. Ferries went across the channel in much the same way as an alcoholic goes over a rope bridge, swaying and lurching and generally making a slow, unpleasant hash of it. The only good thing about the constant nausea was that at least it gave you something to do. Hanging over a rail at least meant that you were out in the open air, occupying yourself. You weren't indoors (or 'portside' or 'noggy' or whatever stupid sailor term they use to mean 'indoors'). You weren't sitting on a bolted-down orange plastic seat drinking some silty coffee. You weren't remembering the 1970s with a tiny can of Double Diamond in the so-called bar. And you weren't trying to sleep on a greasy floor which had been carpeted with left-over British Rail seat-covers and kept lurching along with the boat (or 'ship' or 'jumkiddle', etc.). It was vile, but you knew you were at least on a ferry.

Nowadays it is hard to tell what you are on when you take the ferry.

For a start it is bloody enormous. You wander the corridors, looking for somewhere to sit down. From time to time you encounter the odd ancient mariner, or more likely ancient van driver, looking to tell his boring albatross story to someone. Whole civilizations rise and fall in forgotten corridors. Finally you stumble into a bar. And there is a band on, playing hits of the eighties, and a whole room full of people dancing. It's like being in some sort of New Romantic Tardis. Above you is a cinema. Round the back there is a gym. There's a duty-free shop. A hairdresser's and a games room.

The whole thing is like a wonderful shopping mall, only ten times smaller and not wonderful. The games room in this context means a windowless shed with a Space Invaders machine. The cinema is a windowless shed with a video projection screen that's OK for showing blobby football matches in pubs but less effective when showing the second-rate British 'romcom' you've seen three times already. The hairdresser is a former purser turned to drink. And the duty-free shop just sells overpriced booze and perfume that's cheaper in France and more drinkable (the booze, not the perfume).

But there are so many things to do and the place is such a labyrinth that the chances are when the ferry gets to the other side of the Channel no one will notice and everyone will just go back across the water again, dancing to Duran Duran, playing video games, having their hair done. And again, and again, until their families forget them and the ports close from lack of use.

AIRPORT TERMINALS

There's a reason they're called terminals. You may well die there. Can there be any place more airless, more dankly lit, more depressing, soul-destroying and psyche-eating than an airport terminal? They are, essentially, great big dungeons with neon signs and trolleys (see *Luggage trolleys*). People who do the PR for them say that terminals are like towns. Yes, if that town is Crappyville, Ontario. They use labels like 'The Gatwick Village'. Once upon a

There's a reason they're called terminals. You may well die there.

time there *was* a Gatwick village. It had a pond and a little church. The current Gatwick Village has neither of these things, unless a box in the basement counts as a church and a leak near Burger King surrounded by those annoying yellow plastic easels saying WARNING: WET SURFACE counts as a pond. If, as they claim, this sterile island of shops, fake pubs and yellow plastic easels is the Gatwick Village, then that makes the people who run it Gatwick Village idiots.

AIRPORT PARKING

You won't be able to, unless you have brought a gold ingot with you. Long-stay parking is so expensive that some people, just for the hell of it, put their car in short stay so they can at least choose to be ripped off. Instead of leaving your car in the 'long-stay car park', why not save money by having it converted into a small jet plane and fly yourself abroad?

There's also the distance factor. Be sure and leave home as early as possible, because the car park is nowhere near the actual terminal. In fact it is so far away from the airport that, as you park, take a look out of the window. Rather than the airport terminal, you will have a better chance of seeing your own house and, in it, the neighbours, sharing your brandy with some burglars.

AIRPORT STAFF

～

Working in an airport cannot be healthy. Like railway stations or motorway services, airport terminals aren't really places; they are things you leave from to go to places. As a consequence, the people who work there seem to have left part of their identity somewhere else. Like the stupid character in the useless film about the halfwit man who lived in a terminal (whatever that was called), airport staff seem trapped in a limbo where everyone else is arriving and departing. Airport staff – grey-skinned, slow and deeply sullen – are also the reason it takes half an hour to get a cup of tea at the 'food concession'.

Airport staff are, however, not to be confused with airline ground staff. Dodos to their eagle-like colleagues in the actual aeroplanes, ground staff get to wear the same uniforms, the same fake tans and the same fake smiles, but never get off the ground. While their co-workers fly the friendly skies, visiting glamorous locations on a daily basis, and do it with pilots as well, the ground staff are stuck behind. They sit behind what are effectively giant tills – there's even a set of scales, just like in Waitrose – and spend their lives repeating themselves to idiots

Dodos to their eagle-like colleagues in the actual aeroplanes, ground staff get to wear the same uniforms, the same fake tans and the same fake smiles, but never get off the ground.

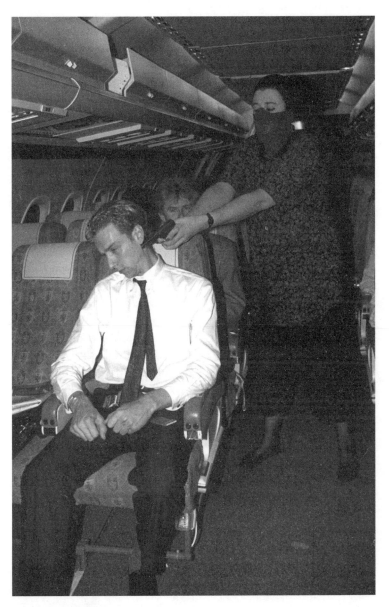

Another wonderful day in economy.

with too much baggage. You are going on holiday; they are going home to Purley. Therefore they do not give a toss if you want a window or an aisle seat. They couldn't care less if you ordered a vegetarian in-flight meal. And they are about as excited as a sloth in a coma over the news that you do not want to put your laptop in the hold.

Plus they have to ask all those stupid security questions. (See *Stupid security questions*.)

Airports are full of people carrying toy koalas with pilots' helmets, moneyboxes shaped like Bahrain, and Burberry jigsaws.

AIRPORT SHOPS
∽

Not to be confused with duty-free shops (see *Duty-free shops*). Airport shops sell things that nobody really wants but will buy because they are briefly trapped in a terminal with their money and their kids. They can't get rid of their kids by handing them over the counter, so they hand over the money instead. As a result, airports are full of people carrying toy koalas with pilots' helmets, moneyboxes shaped like Bahrain, and Burberry jigsaws.

They also buy 'airport editions' of novels, which are giant paperback versions of books that are only out in hardback. This makes a bookshop look like a sort of giants' Oxfam, as all of the books are the kind that end up in charity shops after the holidays.

Airport shopping areas will always feature at least one of the following:

1   The biggest Dixons in the universe, which, by some paradox, only sells very tiny things.
2   Nine WH Smith's, all about 3 feet away from each other.
3   A shoe shop with a bonkers name like Spnurki or Fagioli & Embolism.

4   A big counter right in the middle that sells caviare and
    champagne and smoked salmon, even though the only people
    who can afford to eat there are currently in the first-class
    lounge, where they get all that for free.

5   A shop that only sells blue envelopes.

6   Three identical shirt shops which all sell bright pink shirts and
    cricket bat cufflinks at £100 a pop.

7   A chemist with a worrying emphasis on tropical disease
    medicines, disinfectant, deep vein thrombosis stockings, first-
    aid kits and defibrillators.

8   A really macho-looking pub, called The Old Shillelagh, with
    five customers, all of whom are having a cup of mint tea.

9   A sort of pizza restaurant that also does Mexican food, and
    pasta, and burgers, staffed by Koreans.

10 A shop that sells anything, so long as it involves teddy bears,
    Union Jacks or fake pub wares. Thus you can get a drunk teddy
    waving a flag, a beer mat displaying a Union Jack-tattooed
    teddy's face or a pint of Teddy Bear's Union Jack lager.

11 A luggagey shop, which only sells luggage accessories, things
    that go on luggage and, in some parts of the world, things that
    look a bit like luggage, such as enormous leather caps.

BUREAU DE CHANGE

In a hurry? Never mind, you'll do it at the other end. Yeah, right.
You can't do it at the other end because you don't know the foreign
word for 'bureau de change', or when you realize that it's probably
'bureau de change' you can't find it, or if you do it's closed, or there's
a revolution on. Do it now.

And when they give you the money, minus their gigantic
commission, and with a handful of chump change – funny how the
change is always puny and the commission always massive, and
never the other way round – do try and remember the exchange
rate. If you can't remember the exchange rate for whatever bizarre

currency it is, there is a simple, if peculiar, formula that may help. When in doubt, multiply either the British money or the foreign money – whichever seems least absurd – by 1.6. This will work in nine cases out of ten, and even in the tenth case it still makes you look knowledgeable.

Beware of change. Outside the three major currencies of the world – which are of course, in reverse order, the dollar, the euro and the pound – any money you are given you will never ever be able to get rid of. That wasn't a quirky collection of foreign coins you found in great-grandad's drawer, it was a load of olden days holiday money he couldn't get rid of. Put it in the charity envelopes on the plane. Make a bear dance for it. Anything.

LUGGAGE TROLLEYS

∾

The mutant cousin of the supermarket trolley, airport luggage trolleys differ from their relatives in that a) you are not meant to keep anything in them for very long, and b) they are even worse. Nothing stays on an airport trolley, except the small bag you have hooked on the hook thing. This stays on purely to bash your knees as you try and control the trolley. After a few minutes of attempting to direct the trolley, when it clearly wants to go and sniff some other trolley's backside, you finally have to give up when it throws all your luggage onto the ground.

Another bizarre fact about trolleys is that, like foreign adaptor plugs (and indeed foreigners), there seems to be no common agreement on what is the best sort of trolley. Some are huge and you can put your aunt on them. Some are so small that they are only fit for taking handbags for a walk. And there is no common braking rule. In parts of Europe and the Far East, squeezing the rod behind the handle means that the trolley will stop. In Britain it won't start unless you squeeze the rod, which releases the brake instead of engaging it.

The whole thing is clearly a device to alert visitors from other lands to the fact that Britain is different to other nations. It is also a clever way to make people who have been in other airports come to an abrupt stop and watch as their designer luggage shoots out at their fellow travellers like matching-buckled bullets.

The kids are in the bottom suitcase.

STUPID SECURITY QUESTIONS

Yes, security is very important. And X-ray machines and identity checks do serve their purpose (especially if that purpose is to protect and irritate the public). But 'security questions' are a different matter. Has any major incident ever been prevented by a member of ground staff asking someone if they packed their bags themselves? Perhaps they are hoping to catch someone out, and that one day a passenger will say, 'No, I use a baggage-packing service run by the PLO.'

Here are a few things that, if you are bored, ratty or just hung over, you can say to liven up (and shorten) your travels:

Q: Did you pack your own bags?

A: I leave that to my manservant, Jeeves. Osama bin Jeeves.

Q: Are you aware of their contents?

A: I keep seventeen identical suitcases in my hall, each one containing a random selection of items. When I travel, I simply grab the nearest one. This one's quite heavy, and it mews.

Q: Have your bags been left unattended at any time?

A: Certainly not. They have their own nanny, and there is a set of phone numbers by the strap if she needs to contact me.

Q: Has anyone asked you to carry any items onto this flight?

A: An old lady asked me to help her with her very large bag, but, knowing airport regulations well, I told her to carry it herself.

Q: Are you carrying any hazardous materials?

A: I've got a couple of Jeffrey Archer novels, if that's what you mean.

GATES

The main thing about gates is that they are never anywhere near where you are. The nearest gate is at least twenty minutes' walk away, and the furthest may involve you calling a taxi. Nobody knows why this is. Perhaps the airlines fear that, if the gate is near the airport exit, passengers who hate flying will change their minds and run away, whereas if the gate is very distant they will think, 'Oh well, I appear to have walked most of the way to my holiday destination, I might as well stay.'

Gates are never, ever, near. Even in tiny airports on little Pacific islands which consist of a tin hut and a runway, the gate is half a mile away, possibly on a different atoll.

Also, gates are numbered according to the same system, oddly, as English streets. This means that gates which, according to their numbers, ought to be adjacent are in fact very far apart. And vice versa. So Gate 2 is half a mile away from Gate 1, while Gate 17 is quite close to Gate 45. And your flight is leaving from Gate 196, and the moving walkway (see *Moving walkways*) isn't working.

Gates are also the final frontier of the airport world and the last chance the airport has to add to your load of travel misery. This is why there is nothing to do at the gate except get a drink from the extremely depressing vending machine. This is why you are always called to the gate about an hour before boarding, so you leave the gay paradise of shops and duty free to spend forty minutes sitting in an area ('room' is too grand a word) full of plastic seats all stuck together so you have to sit across from a load of backpackers who are all listening to the same Dutch rock album on headphones.

MOVING WALKWAYS

The moment you heave yourself and your baggage onto a moving walkway, one of three things will happen:

1 It won't be working, and you will experience a weird sensation of moving backwards without actually moving at all.
2 A fat family will assume that, because the walkway is moving, they can just stand there like tubs of clothing and have a chat. The people behind them who took the moving walkway because

they are late and may miss their flight, and are now stuck behind the fat family, are clearly neurotic fidgets who just need to stop and smell the flowers.

3   Conversely, if you yourself are pushing your trolley down the walkway at a sensible cruising speed, suddenly there will come from behind you the sound of thundering wheels before a man with all the luggage in the world hurtles towards you and knocks you sideways.

THE BLUE ELECTRIC CART THING

For some reason, the beeping alarm on the blue electric cart thing has the opposite effect to that intended. Instead of making you think, 'Oh, there is a blue electric cart thing coming up behind me, I'll step out the way,' the tone of the alarm is so weedy, you think, 'I wonder what that weedy noise is?', and get run over by a blue electric cart thing with two old ladies sitting on the back.

UPGRADES

One of the great urban myths of air travel. 'No, really, it happened to a friend of a friend. Well, their uncle… or their au pair… anyway, it's true. All you have to do is dress nicely and they'll bump you up to first class.'

Maybe, but any time a non-fictional person tries it, this is the result.

'Hello. I'm nicely dressed. Is there any chance of an upgrade?'

'I'm sorry sir, this is a very full flight. Now, if you'll excuse me, I have to check in these badly dressed rock musicians who are all going first class.'

And what about the converse? In an ideal world, first-class passengers who have been unruly would get bumped down to economy. Now that would be worth seeing.

CLASSES

There are subtle differences between each class on planes.

Class	Pros	Cons
Economy	Not actually walking to your destination	Cramped, smelly, loud
Business	Free stuff, bigger seats	Can smell economy class
First	Caviar, bed, free gold crown	Very expensive (but you're not paying)
Cockpit	Get to fly the plane	In later life, have to marry flight attendant

AIRLINE PASSENGERS

1 The family with lots of babies. They always get the front seats in economy, so everyone can hear the screaming and watch them change nappies. The screaming does not stop. Ever.
2 The couple who want to tell you about all the places they have been to. Good Lord, they are well travelled. And, if their dull rants are to be believed, travel has not broadened their minds at all.
3 The snoggers. Get a room! Or go on the wing.
4 The man with BO. Shouldn't they have showers and footbaths before you get on the plane? They do at swimming pools, and you only spend a half hour in those.
5 The important businessman. If you get bored with his incessant tapping on his stupid laptop, wait until he goes for a wee, then delete all his files.

SHORT FLIGHTS

Short plane journeys used to be delightful. A small breakfast, a quick journey, a nice coffee, and there you were in Paris or

Edinburgh or Dublin, refreshed. But then some fool invented the super-budget flight. Without unnecessary overheads, the logic runs, flights can be cheaper and more convenient. In reality, cheap flights are now horrible experiences. With no tickets, passengers all bundle onto the plane, all trying to sit at the front, and all ending up at the back. With no complimentary food or 'beverages', everyone has to fork out huge sums of money for the kind of in-flight dining experience that only the cast of *Grange Hill* might enjoy. The whole thing is roughly akin to a school coach trip, except that nobody is going to swap you their Breakaway bar for a couple of Jaffa cakes.

LONG FLIGHTS
~

O nly tolerable in first class (see Classes). This is because airliners are essentially old-fashioned cruise liners with wings. They maintain the strict hierarchy and caste system mentality that served the *Lusitania* and the *Titanic*. While economy may not be full of cheerful Irish farm workers dancing a jig at 20,000 feet, first class is still an epic luxury fest of champagne, caviare and slightly larger seats. Although, frankly, after seven hours in a jet, all most people really care about is the slightly larger seat. Cramped in economy, with a Norwegian insomniac kicking you in the back and a baby learning to scream in front of you, you can only dream of having a seat with room for more than the one buttock. Meanwhile, in first class, passengers recline on giant *chaises-*

The man on the right is dead and has elected to be buried in first class.

longues like ancient Romans, with cabin staff dropping grapes into their mouths.

REALLY LONG FLIGHTS

There are two theories on how to cope with a really long flight:

1 Get drunk.
2 Don't get drunk.

Try and achieve some sort of balancing act between the two, and you should be all right.

BAGGAGE CAROUSEL

This is one of the cruellest perversions of language ever. A carousel is a lovely thing, all lights and music and happy children hanging on to gaudy wooden horses. It is not a bunch of rubber slats flapping round a depressing hall in the bowels of an airport. Give a happy child a busted suitcase or a crushed holdall to ride and it will cry. Carousels resemble many other things found in a fairground – ghost train, dodgems, helter skelter – but not a pretty merry-go-round. Misery-go-round, perhaps.

There is a sad and predictable routine to waiting at the baggage carousel. You arrive, full of hope and knackeredness, and eventually find which empty carousel claims to be hosting your luggage today. You find a place to stand, banging several people's ankles with your dodgy trolley, and wait around, listening to the dead slap of rubber as nobody's bags appear.

After twenty minutes, just when you are wondering if you can manage without any luggage, a bag comes down the chute. It is not a happy bag. Someone appears to have tried to open it with a mallet. It has been repaired with three kinds of sticky tape, some of which

'That's ours... oh no it isn't... that's ours... oh no... that's ours... no...'

partially obscures the word FRAGILE.

This bag is followed, a while later, by the biggest plastic suitcase you have ever seen. It is so big that it looks more like a car than a suitcase. Designed to be impregnable, it makes a rattling sound when its owner heaves it off the carousel.

After that it's a free for all, as bags, cases, holdalls and backpacks come tumbling out like incompetent parachutists. None of them are yours. You pass the time by noting the wide variety of items on the carousel. Most impressive of all is what seems to be an entire washing machine in a bin liner.

You grow desperate. You start to eye people up who have similar baggage to yours. Perhaps they have stolen your luggage. Perhaps the baggage handlers are even now going through your bag, dressing themselves up in your wife's clothes and laughing at your choice of holiday reading.

Finally, everyone else has gone apart from a tiny, intense woman in a cagoule, and six priests. There is silence. And then a mighty thud as the last bag is hurled onto the carousel. You move towards

Baggage handlers are even now going through your bag, dressing themselves up in your wife's clothes and laughing at your choice of holiday reading.

it. The woman in the cagoule moves towards it. You step back. It's not your bag.

Leaving the baggage area to seek consolation in whisky, you hear a tiny, far-off thump. It is your bag. Most of it …

DUTY FREE

Duty free is the place where things you don't want are available at prices you still can't afford, but you buy them anyway because they're cheaper than normal, a small bit. In the old days everyone went to duty free for the fags, but since we are now a bit more health-conscious nation people just go for the booze. This they are discerning about, and only buy spirits, especially whisky, which some people must think can only be purchased at airports. They did plan to get some perfume for the wife, but they are foiled as a) there are

more than three kinds, b) even the kind that she likes comes in thirty-four different kinds, and c) for the price of a bottle the size of a mink's eye they could buy a house in Runcorn. So in the end the wife gets a pointlessly huge Toblerone, which makes her feel fat.

Beautiful gifts you'll want to keep... the receipt for.

THEM AND US

THEM

THE GERMANS
~

The first thing to bring up, relentlessly, again and again, is the war. Germans are, quite reasonably, sick of us going on about the war (that is, for younger readers, the Second World War, the one the Americans think they won). German people don't understand that the war is the last thing we as a nation won. They can't see that it's not personal – well, it *is* personal – but we are not only a nation whose imperial glories and global importance are long gone, but we are a petty and small-minded nation whose imperial glories and global importance are long gone. Besides, we

And they say Germans have no sense of humour.

beat them. Twice. And we won the 1966 World Cup. Just because they rebuilt their country from nothing in 1945, became an efficient and sensible member of the world community and won the World Cup three times, they think they're something special.

But if we can leave the war to one side for a moment (That's the 1939–45 war, not, as some people think, the 1941–45 war. Anybody could have won a war that short.), it's worth reflecting that Germany is a very bad holiday destination. For a start, it has the most useless holiday coastline in the world. Germany is a very big country – it ought to be, since it is two perfectly reasonable 1970s' countries stuck together – and it has lakes and mountains and

Germany is a very big country – it ought to be, since it is two perfectly reasonable 1970s' countries stuck together.

forests and lots of very Germanic things, but it is sod-all useless when it comes to going to the beach. This is why no Germans have ever swum off their own coasts, and this is why Germans love going on holidays abroad. And you can see their point. There's something very… well, *woody* about going on holiday in Germany. Pine trees and log cabins and beer-drenched trestle tables and stout walking sticks… Germans have a very close relationship with wood. And most Germans, after a few months, probably think, 'I'm a bit fed up with all this wood, I think I'll go on holiday. Either that or drive up and down the autobahn at 300 kph.'

German cities are also not always appealing. Many German cities have beautiful architecture and fine cathedrals and museums, but many others, frankly, don't. An afternoon in, say, Dusseldorf is like being in some sort of Middlesbrough that's come into some money. It's not all Brandenburg Gates and Unter Den Linden.

Germans do, it must be said, react well to tourists. They are friendly. They are helpful. They have learned the language (which is tourist lingo for 'They speak English'). And, most importantly, they are prepared to dress up for us. Either as rural, peasanty types

This man was born looking like this.

in leather shorts or flowery frocks, or, in the case of the hotel trade, strange sort of alpine guides with rimless specs and those collarless jackets that the Beatles wore in the early part of their career.

They are, famously, efficient. This is good if you want your towels changed (Germans are very good with towels) but bad when it comes to totting up what you had from the minibar.

It is only when Germans go on holiday themselves that the other side of the national persona comes out – the side that is funny about sunbeds. The German attitude to other people's sunbeds is much the same as that of their grandparents to other people's countries: annexation. Not to be stereotypical, but Germans at home and in their daily lives are calm, friendly, intelligent people whose energies are mostly channelled into the purchase of bizarre rimless spectacles and CDs by David Hasselhof. They are not notably obsessive.

But give a German a beach, swimming pool, terrace or anything where there might be some kind of lounger, sunbed or reclining seat and he turns into a towel fetishist with obsessive-compulsive disorder. You come down to the pool after a sumptuous brekker, ready for some serious lying-down-until-lunchtime. And there it is, on the sunbed, like a white fluffy dog doo. A towel. Pristine, creaseless, and obviously purchased solely to put on a sunbed. (In all-German resorts, the sunbed towel has probably evolved in an entirely symbolic fashion, and to secure a sunbed in a German resort you merely have to put down anything vaguely towelesque, like a face flannel, or even a Kleenex.)

Why are they so obsessed with claiming a place on the sunbeds? Do they look at the rest of the holidaymakers the night before, or perhaps on the flight over, and think, 'Hmm. This bunch look suntan crazy. I'd better reserve a sunbed otherwise I'll have to stand by the pool all day'? Is there a stereotype of the English in Germany that is the polar opposite, where German stand-up comedians do jokes about how you'd better claim your sunbed with a towel otherwise the rest of the world will use it as a table for their lager? Perhaps they think we steal the sunbeds. Maybe they think we sleep under them.

Whatever it is, it's a national obsession. One merely wonders if they had it in the former East Germany too; the idea of angry Romanians coming down to the pool at a far-away Black Sea resort and finding a lot of cheap towels with *Wilkommen im Leipziger Traktorfest* printed on them all over the sunbeds is somehow hard for the human mind to tolerate.

THE FRENCH
᷈

The French are not the same as Parisians. Parisians are very rude, the Cockneys in many ways of their land, and if you try and speak French to them they will just stare at you, as one might stare at a monkey that has learned French.

The rest of France is not nearly as bad, but there are many peculiarities native to les Français. Not least of which is their belief that the best kind of holidays are a) those with something of a peasant flavour, and b) those which cost about a billion euros.

In other lands, the expensive holidays and the peasanty ones are very different. You spend a week in a nice hotel, you pay the nice hotel rate. You spend a week in a roofless hovel, you pay the roofless hovel rate. Simple. And yet the French, in their quirky way, do not agree. If you have, for some reason, travelled to Normandy to spend a week in a roofless hovel, you will pay a fortune to do so.

If you try and speak French to them they will just stare at you, as one might stare at a monkey that has learned French.

Perhaps the French are so proud of their enormous yet strangely unpopulated land that they feel it's all worth top dollar to tourists. Perhaps they love it so much that they really cannot differentiate between L'Hotel Empereur Splendide du Monde d'Or and Madame Odeureuse's old pigsty with a tarpaulin over it.

Either way, within minutes of arriving at your French holiday destination you will learn a valuable lesson in the French language:

This man has been surgically altered to look Frencher.

'picturesque' does not mean 'like a lovely picture', it means 'take a picture of this place, and then try and make someone believe that it cost you £200 a day'.

Outside of the tourist trade, the French do not go around acting oddly, much. When not driving mopeds disguised as vans, dressing as burglars with loaves of bread under their arms, or voting for men called Valérie, the French are actually quite a normal nation. Like us, they watch TV and go to discos. Like us, they don't speak any other languages and they don't get on with the Germans. And like us, they are fond of wine (the fact that French wine is served in little baby glasses and the wine we drink is served in buckets says, of course, nothing about the British).

But unlike us, the French go a bit funny when they go on their *vacances*. If you meet a Brit on holiday, he or she is likely to be at the very least a friendly sort. He or she may even embrace you and declare that you are his or her best mate, you are. Other nationalities are equally, if not more, friendly. The Germans, too, are friendly, so long as they have established that you are not interested in their sunbeds. However, on holiday the French go all – to use one of their own words – cliquey.

You have met the French couple in the hotel. They are quite pleasant. They tell you their names and everything. At the pool they laugh politely when the fat kid falls in. They share their tanning lotions. All is well. And yet… and yet when you see them going out in the morning, and you ask them out of mild interest where they are off to – they shrug. They frown, a little. Could it be that they have forgotten? Perhaps they are confused? Not so. They are going somewhere better. They have found something interesting to do. You will be spending the morning pricing flippers in the Thievomart. They will be drinking Brandy Alexanders with Roman Polanski. Of course, this is all paranoid nonsense (apart from the bit about the flippers). They are doing no such thing. They are, for all you really know, going to sit in the dried-out local park drinking Strongbow. But they have managed to give the impression that they are doing something better than what you are doing.

This is, it may be fair to say, a French skill. Only the French – who after all invented the phrase 'savoir faire', which sort of implies that they are the only ones who savoir how to faire anything – can make you feel that what you are doing is a bit pants whereas what they are doing is toptastic.

The fact that at 7 that night you are driving to a Michelin-starred seafood restaurant when you see the French couple sitting outside Burger King with a bag of onion rings between them still does not make it better. They know something you don't, and that's it.

THE SPANISH

After their civil war, the Spanish endured the Fascist yoke of General Franco for many years. When he died, democracy was reintroduced, along with very lax dope-smoking laws and a lot of gay bars. Spain was a cool place to be once more. With ridiculous cathedrals, trendy museums and a bemusing attitude of tolerance to Union-Jack-faced beer men, Spain has long been a relaxed place.

Not half it hasn't. Getting a plumber in Spain is reputedly harder than getting a peerage. Punctuality is a concept so distant from the Hispanic mindset that suddenly all those wobbly clocks in Salvador Dali paintings begin to make sense; Dali wasn't being surreal, he was just trying to explain the Spanish attitude to time.

Punctuality is a concept so distant from the Hispanic mindset that suddenly all those wobbly clocks in Salvador Dali paintings begin to make sense.

The Spanish famously gave the world the concept of '*mañana*', which means, literally, 'I can't be arsed'. Their working hours are bizarre beyond belief; they all take the afternoon off for a siesta, or kip. This is apparently because it is so hot that no work is possible – a concept that has not only survived the invention of air-conditioning, but also applies to the cold, coastal north of Spain. Anyone who has endured a wet Tuesday afternoon in, say, Santander, wandering around trying to find a bar or a café that's not run by the temporarily comatose, knows how feeble an excuse siesta can be.

Apparently, and this is a fact, in the post-EU world of the twenty-first century there are plans afoot to abolish the siesta. Productivity will increase, Spain will come into line with the rest of the world, and no longer will a walk round the town centre in the afternoon resemble a scene in a Western just prior to a two-man gunfight.

On the other hand, you still won't be able to get a plumber.

THE ITALIANS

∾

A warning from history: Italy, like Britain, used to be the mightiest empire the world had ever seen. Their empire, however, was the Roman one, which has been defunct for over 1,500 years. The British one has only been defunct for fifty years, but we should heed

Despite his claims to the contrary, this man has the genitals of a tsetse fly.

the Italian example. In about 1,000 years from now the British are going to stop being noble, firm-jawed stoics whose language unites the globe, and become long-haired lads in cheap leather jackets who ride around on scooters wolf-whistling at any woman who is not actually their mother.

Italians gave the world some of its greatest painters, sculptors and thinkers. It may not be a coincidence that most of these great men were also homosexuals. The heterosexual Italian seems so blinded by the idea of rumpo that he can think of little else. Italy's leader made his money out of pornography, and for a while a porn star called La Cicciolina was an Italian MP. The whole nation is clearly obsessed with smut, and their only hope for survival as a country is to become entirely gay.

THE DUTCH

Maybe it was being owned by Spain for so long that gave the Dutch their taste for marijuana. Maybe it was all those heavy Protestant ministers that made them rebel and install brothels on every street corner. Either way, the Dutch are the super-liberal experiment of Europe, the model leisure culture. It is not actually clear what normal people in cities like Amsterdam do for a living; they can't all be drug dealers.

Of course, the reason they can spend all their free time smoking spliffs while cycling round to the dirty magazine shop on ecstasy is because there are no hills in Holland, and so they won't get knackered. Life is easy in Holland, unless you fall into a canal.

The other thing about the Dutch is that they all speak English. This is perhaps because they are scared that one day the world will notice that the Dutch language is essentially German pronounced a bit more twangily.

THE BELGIANS

The Argos Dutch. Belgians have a hard time, being divided into Flamands and Walloons. There can never have been two stupider names for an ethnic group. Swallows and Amazons would have been better. This terrible fact has scarred the Belgian psyche, as has the depressing nature of their cultural heritage. The two most famous Belgians – Tintin and Hercule Poirot – are not even real people, while their most famous piece of art is a statue of a toddler urinating. These things can get to you after a while.

SCANDINAVIANS

Divided, of course, into several nations, many of whom it is hard for the ignorant tourist to tell apart. Denmark appears

Cycling and marijuana – every Dutchman's dream combination.

to be part of Scandinavia, even though it is small and green and the other Scandinavian nations are huge and white. It is possible that Denmark has been classified as Scandinavian so that people from Norway and Sweden can go there and buy beer. Norwegians and Swedes are very fond of beer, which traditionally is very expensive in their homelands. This is good news for the Danes, whose tiny country is every weekend overrun with well-mannered, blond heavy drinkers.

Norway and Sweden are very different countries too. Sweden is very clean and scary, a sort of Canada of Scandinavia. Sweden makes a scary clean car, the Volvo, a great big scary jet fighter called the Saab Draken, and is also of course the home of Abba and Ikea, surely the two cleanest examples of, respectively, pop music and home furnishings ever (and Abba may qualify as both pop music and home furnishings).

Norway is quite different. For a kick-off it used to belong to Sweden, and there was much fighting to get it back to being Norwegian again. Norway is not famous for any cars or jets, its home furnishings are literally that – being heavy, wood-carved items that you could hurt someone with – and its music scene, while thriving, does include one of the least chart-friendly genres in rock, namely Norwegian death metal. Do not confuse Norway with Sweden, or you may get a chair through your head.

As for the Finns, they spent centuries being very nervous on account of being on the Russian border. They make great movies and drink more than anybody else. Researchers are still too frightened to find out what music Finns like.

THE RUSSIANS

Russia in the twentieth century used to be a great place for a holiday if you liked little tin badges with pictures of Soviet leaders on (at one point these were so fashionable that it seemed as though every clod had a silver Lenin) or if you enjoyed queuing. Nowadays it seems to have become a sort of Sopranoskis theme park. Russians used to be enormous, melancholy figures who drank to forget oppression. An evening in a Russian bar would generally end with a very large man in a fur hat weeping into his, and your, vodka. The yoke of Communist oppression weighed heavily on the Russian soul. Now there isn't any Communism and they all want it back again. Either that, or they are riding round in armour-plated SUVs pretending to be, or actually being, gangsters.

It's hardly Dostoevsky, is it? It's not very Chekhovian: 'Mother, I must go back to the cherry orchard.' 'Wait a bit dear. Some men are making Uncle Vanya an offer he can't refuse.'

Right: 'What do we want? Ruthless authoritarian crushing of the human spirit! When do we want it? Now!'

THE JAPANESE

The Japanese are a polite, shy race whose interests include violent pornography, graphic horror movies and watching two fat men in jockstraps knock each other down. They are famous for their traditional crafts and the quiet serenity of their Zen-related arts. They are also famous for hi-fi, DVD, video games and absolutely enormous tellies.

The visitor to Japan will probably never see the rural, traditional Japan. This is because it is almost completely inaccessible. True, the Japanese commuter can be back in his home village within the hour, but the Western tourist cannot, because the Western tourist can't

Warning – scooter does not transform into giant robot.

The Japanese are a polite, shy race whose interests include violent pornography, graphic horror movies and watching two fat men in jockstraps knock each other down.

speak any Japanese and the man at Tokyo Central Station doesn't seem to speak any English. And all the signs are in those weird letters you normally only see on the side of model tank kits, and when you ask someone a question they just giggle. You can't get any lunch because of the language barrier, so you just go to McDonald's and point at things. When the girls behind the counter have stopped giggling, you find you have ordered an apple pie and a Homer Simpson glove-puppet, so you go back to the hotel and watch a game show whose rules, aim and logic are completely beyond you.

The Japanese at home are, like some other nations (see *The Germans*, *The French*), very different when they travel. For a kick-off, they are kings of tourism. Next to Americans (see *Americans*) the Japanese are the super-tourists of the modern age. When we think of the word 'tourist', in fact, we are just as likely to imagine some Nikon-happy party of Japanese people, one of whom is wearing a hat with a tiny umbrella on top, as we are a lot of American men called Hiram J Snorkenburger the XIVth with huge tartan jacksies.

And like Americans, Japanese people do have special clothes for travelling. At home they wear either the kimono or the Paul Smith suit. But once freed of the restraints of the homeland they seem to head as one for the King's Road and kit themselves out in a bewildering array of trendy gear. Dyed blue hair, black T-shirts, enormous climbing boots, kilts, jackets with cartoon animals on the back... this is the uniform of the Japanese tourist abroad. It looks mental in any situation, except for walking through London, where it looks sort of normal.

The other very important thing to know about the Japanese is that they are mad keen on toilets (see *Toilets*).

AUSTRALIANS

Many Australians don't like the British. This is apparently because we complain a lot. We are 'whingeing Poms'. Australians love to complain about how the British love moaning. They rarely stop to wonder what we are moaning about – probably being in Australia, a land where they nearly wiped out the indigenous population but have managed to lovingly preserve thousands of species of poisonous insects and reptiles.

Australia is a new country that likes to have votes on whether it should have the same Queen as us. They always come close to abolishing the Queen and replacing her with democracy or something, but always change their minds at the last minute. This is clearly an attention-getting device, one designed to alert royalty to their existence, so Prince Charles has to be sent over to be shot at again.

Australians love to complain about how the British love moaning.

Australians make genial hosts, or think they do, with their enormous reliance on 'bluffness' and 'speaking their minds'. This seems to largely consist of making bluff remarks about what a fool you are, or speaking their minds in a negative, perhaps critical way. It's weird how plain-speaking people always find it difficult to speak plainly in a positive manner.

On vacation, Australian geniality is enormous. Whether sitting on Eros wondering where Piccadilly Circus might be, or working behind all the bars of the capital city, Australians fit right in. They love coming to Britain because it is full of Australian bars, all featuring Australian beers, Australian entertainments, and Australians.

NEW ZEALANDERS

Less cheerful than Australians, New Zealanders come from a country which until recently exactly resembled Britain in 1956. The principal mode of transport was the Morris Minor, there wasn't much on the telly, and people were overly fond of rugby.

This may be the reason why so many New Zealanders on holiday here can be seen strolling about, gazing about them in wonder at the technological miracles of the early twenty-first century. Either that, or they're all drunk because they have won the bastard rugby again.

In America, the prime function of New Zealanders is to be mistaken for English people.

SOUTH AFRICANS
∽

Known among backpackers as 'the nation that used to pretend it was someone else on holiday'. Until the release of Nelson Mandela from his long incarceration South Africans were the holiday scum of Europe, pariahs of inter-railing. With their strange accents, part Dutch, part Cyberman, they were easy to spot. Their curious attitude to racial matters preceded them, but their apparent belief that some peoples were inferior to others was agreed on by all, although it was the South Africans everyone felt were the inferior ones. Soon you would hear South Africans claiming that they were in fact from New Zealand or some nicer country, just to have someone to talk to.

Nowadays, of course, all South Africans despise racism and they are among the most liberal of rich, white, privileged tourists.

CANADIANS
∽

There are two Canadas: the English-speaking, enormously butch, plaid-shirted Canada where they chop down the mighty peckerwood and drink maple syrup from the tree, and the French-speaking, enormously butch, plaid-shirted Canada, where they etc. etc. Visitors to Canada from abroad often have to stop and try to remember which bit they are in, as Canada is in reality such a big, clean, nice place that looks a bit like America after a long hot bath, and it seems to lack not so much an ethnic character as, well, any character.

Canadians get very annoyed about this, because they are very keen not to have their culture assimilated by the United States. They also like to deny that they say 'oot' instead of 'out', that their policemen all dress in red jodhpurs with enormous old-fashioned Scout hats on their heads, and that they invented Bryan Adams.

But Canada cannot help being what it is, which is deeply nice. For example, despite the years of struggle for recognition of the French language, if you wander into a Montreal bar and say, 'Bonjour', which is only polite, you are then entitled to conduct the rest of your conversation in English. This is not only rational and considerate of the locals, but is about as un-French as you can get. Imagine doing the same thing in a Parisian bar. Wouldn't happen.

Canadians are rarely seen abroad, or at least rarely noticed, probably because everyone mistakes them for quietly spoken Americans who say 'oot' instead of 'out'.

AMERICANS
∼

We all know about oppressed minorities. The United States of America, however, seems to have become the world's first oppressed majority. They are so unpopular that even the French – who are famous for not doing what anyone else does, even if it hurts – have laid aside their international bloody-mindedness and Jerry Lewis DVDs and said that, yes, they too do not like the Americans.

The 'special relationship' that Britain has with the USA does not seem to have helped UK–US relations, either. A Prime Minister who expressed enthusiasm for a US President is labelled his 'poodle' (yeah, like an American President would own a French dog). Anyone who dares to say to someone 'Have a nice day' is mocked as a US-made simpleton. And only homosexual dance acts are allowed to dress as cowboys, Native Americans, traffic cops or any other rugged figures from US culture.

There are several bad reasons for not liking Americans. The main one is a kind of post-imperial jealousy. We used to rule the world, now America rules it. Like a former Doctor Who watching his

Ah, the American Cultural Attaché.

successor cock it up, we shake our heads and claim that we used to do it better, or less imperially, or more quietly. We see America invading people and bombing people and trampling on their cultures and not even knowing what country they're in, and instead of thinking, 'Ah, bless, we were like that once,' we get annoyed.

Then again, Americans are mighty strange. When you visit the USA you are traditionally supposed to be impressed by the exuberance of the place. Huge buildings lance the sky. Cars are all yellow and honking. People seem to be a little bit more awake than in Europe. The whole experience is a bit like giving Europe too much coffee.

The people you meet are friendly and helpful. They are curious about your accent (no, you are not from New Zealand) and they are completely uninformed about your homeland. While they don't actually think that you are on speaking terms with the Queen, and no longer address every Brit with 'What ho, old chap, eh?' while screwing in an imaginary monocle, many Americans will bombard you with a selection of nouns and phrases to demonstrate their small store of British information. This is meant to be friendly, but it can be very disconcerting to have someone suddenly bark 'Manchester United!' or 'Bloody hell!' or some other phrase remembered from a backpacking holiday in the 1980s. It is wrong to berate a nation for their well-meaningness and their friendliness. On the other hand, it can make you want to push the whole lot of them into the Grand Canyon.

Mostly the problem is that Americans do not seem to know where anywhere else is. This is particularly galling to the rest of the world, who thanks to Hollywood movies know where every single town, parking lot and fishing hole is in America. Every non-American on Earth can point out New York, Los Angeles and quite possibly Anklemunch, Nebraska, on a map. Yet is the reverse true? No. The reverse is not true.

Americans think that Scotland is in England. They think that London is in Wales. They cannot tell the difference between Britain and Ireland. They are unable to distinguish between an Australian accent and an English accent. (They can just about do an Irish accent, but any attempt at a Scots accent sounds, oddly enough, like Marlon Brando chewing a set of bagpipes.)

This explains why, whenever you take a taxi in America, the driver cannot understand why you do not know his aunt's cousin in Newcastle. The fact that you are from a tiny valley in Wales and have never been outside your homeland before does not faze him. You are clearly English, or British, or something, and you must know his aunt's cousin in Newcastle.

This is faintly excusable when one considers the sheer size of the USA – in American terms Newcastle is next door to Llangobridoch or Land's End mere inches from John O'Groats – but Americans are not fazed in their inaccurateness by any kind of distance. They think France is near Greece, that Poland is down by Italy, and that the Middle East really is in the middle of the east. It's actually worse with non-white races: all nations between Israel and India are 'Arabs', and the religion of Islam belongs to them all.

Americans do have a deeply America-centric view of the world. This is why they always add that ridiculous suffix to the names of towns. London, England. Rome, Italy. Paris, France. Not only does this enable people to match cities with their nations, but it also sorts out the terrible confusion that might cause, say, airline pilots to fly to London, Indiana, Paris, Texas, or Rome, Alaska. The early settlers are to blame for all this. They would see a big swamp with a lot of alligators in it and declare that the whole area was now called Birmingham, thereby giving lateral thinking a very bad name. (One wonders how far this system extends. 'Do we have to say Novosibirsk, Russia?' 'Yes, otherwise folks might get it confused with Novosibirsk in Massachusetts.')

Americans also do this thing where, having politely asked you lots of questions about your homeland, they start to quiz you about British perceptions of America. This is where a big neon sign that flashes the word MINEFIELD ought to start going off in your head. Be careful not to express any opinion that may cause offence to, say, a hypersensitive cocaine fiend with a chip on their shoulder. Any divergence from this will result in being told that if you don't like it

America – where anyone can become President, and often does.

here, buddy, you can go back to where you came from. It is pointless to tell them that you do like it here and, indeed, you have always planned to go home where you came from.

Perhaps this chippiness is caused by the very thing that everyone thinks is good about America, namely the whole melting-pot/give-me-your-poor-and-homeless thing. America is built on immigration. Ellis Island is rightly fêted as a gateway to new hope. Yet, for a land founded on immigration, America is not fond of immigrants. For a land whose language – English – is an import, it is not keen on new languages.

Right-wing American commentators like to claim that soon

everyone in America will be speaking only Spanish. Given that we are also told that fairly soon the rest of the world will be speaking only English, this should make the future very interesting. Instead of being understood all round the world, American tourists will have to go to Spanish-speaking countries for their holidays. That'll learn 'em.

Americans on holiday are different to Americans at home. They still maintain high levels of politeness and enthusiasm, but they do so in a warier, somewhat perplexed manner. The youth of America see the world as an obstacle course that only extreme defensiveness and a credit card can keep at bay. Anyone who has trawled through the weblogs, or online diaries, or world-wide whinges, of young American backpackers will be familiar with their overly suspicious attitude. Phrases like 'The carriage was full of people after our money' and 'The biggest problem with Spain is that they all speak Spanish' crop up again and again.

Older Americans, who were perhaps in Europe during the war, or who have seen some Hugh Grant films, are a bit less silly about world travel. Not all of them restrict their tours to visits to the great Starbucks of London, or the McDonald's of Rome, or indeed the Disneyland of Paris. They are here to see art and culture, and in doing so they shame our own tourists, who go abroad to find stronger lagers. But American tourists find the world difficult. And they find Britain particularly difficult. This is because we have tricked them into thinking that we speak English. We do, but we speak the wrong kind of English.

Americans sally forth from their giant hotels, confident that they will not need phrasebooks. If they travel by taxi, they should be all right, and the cabbies reassure them by staying in character, and actually saying things like 'Where to, guv?' and 'A tip? You're a gent and no mistake.' Unfortunately everything else is disorienting. Street signs and place

The British are constantly amazed that Americans cannot pronounce simple, phonetically spelled words like 'Worcestershire', 'Featherstonehaugh' and 'Kirkcudbright'.

names are incomprehensible jumbles of letters. The British are constantly amazed that Americans cannot pronounce simple, phonetically spelled words like 'Worcestershire', 'Featherstonehaugh' and 'Kirkcudbright'. Americans struggle with our difficult money – that old 100 pence to the pound thing can be pretty confusing, especially if you're from a country where they reckon things 100 cents to the dollar. And in the end you will find even the most gallant and adventurous of American tourists standing in Burger King, realizing they cannot understand a single word the person serving them is saying.

US

BRITAIN

This is a concept designed specifically to make life easier for tourists. 'British' is a word we use to describe people who are from the British Isles, but who are not necessarily English. 'British' also means people who are English. 'Britain' does not include Ireland, but 'The British Isles' does. 'Great Britain' is not the same as 'The British Isles' but it is the same as 'Britain'. 'Great British' is a term only used in connection with advertising sausages, or breakfasts. 'British Telecom' is a French telephone company.

It's easy when you know how.

IRELAND

Ireland has long reinvented itself as a great tourist destination. The green fields, the craggy coast… the place is perfect for anyone who wants to visit a giant Cornwall full of Guinness. It does tend to attract the worst kind of boring tourist, the sort of person who wants to 'get back to their roots'. No matter that their roots were probably working in a cotton mill in Leicester, for some reason Ireland acts as a pratmagnet for these people. In between them and various Americans tracing imaginary ancestors, the place can get pretty busy.

Then there's Dublin. Once a small Georgian city much like Bath, Dublin is now a thriving modern community with lots of things made out of glass everywhere. And with Ireland's special tax haven status, Dublin is also of course a major meeting point for artists. Or 'rock stars', as they also like to be known. This means that Ireland is now full of leather-panted clowns in wraparound sunglasses who get up at lunchtime and go to bed at 4. As a result the character of the whole nation has changed. You have to go hundreds of miles to find an authentic, peat-fire-using, Gaelic-speaking community, and even then it's probably a bunch of ecotourists from Leicester getting back to their roots.

You cannot move outside Ireland for Irish pubs, Irish films, Irish film soundtracks and Irish rock groups. The only way to get away from all this tosh is to visit Ireland

Ireland is unique among all the countries that make up the British Isles in that it is fashionable. England was briefly fashionable in the mid-1960s, Scotland enjoyed its moment of hipness in the late nineteenth century, and Wales has got the Super Furry Animals and the Manic Street Preachers, but Ireland seems to be something of a trendstone. You cannot move outside Ireland for Irish pubs, Irish films, Irish film soundtracks and Irish rock groups. The only way to get away from all this tosh is to visit Ireland, where many people got sick of it years before you did.

Northern Ireland is, tourists should note, quite a different place. They spurn the euro, they have very few members of sunglasses-wearing rock bands there, and they very much do not take kindly to tourists who get their religions muddled. It is easy to work out where you are, politically, on account of the many murals and painted kerbstones that local people have thoughtfully painted to let visitors know when to shut up.

This man has been surgically altered to look Irisher.

But the whole place is so sickeningly verdant and friendly and full of beer that after a while you suspect the whole thing is a plot to defraud the EU of valuable funds. And, in a way, it is.

THE WELSH

'Come home to a real fire … buy a holiday cottage in Wales.' The Welsh have not always enjoyed being a tourist nexus, to say the least. Nowadays things are much improved, although Welsh language signs seem designed as much to annoy foreign visitors as to illuminate Welsh drivers, and the not-very-exciting Welsh Assembly will never be a thrilling place for people to visit.

Wales, like all great nations, is divided into two, the North where everyone goes to chapel, speaks Welsh, and is related to someone who once owned a cow, and the South, where none of this applies. The North is bleak and picturesque, and was a major inspiration for that bloke who wrote *Lord of the Rings*. The South has more discos. They are not easy to confuse.

Welsh people have a reputation for taciturnity and volubility, no mean feat. They have produced many great entertainers, rock groups and politicians, and they are responsible for making Patagonia even more unusual than it might have been. There can be no more disorienting moment than realizing that not only have you for some reason booked your holiday on a desolate plain in South America, but all the locals speak Welsh.

Welsh people hate being called 'Taffy' because Taffy was the name of a Welshman who, astonishingly, was also a thief.

THE SCOTS

One of the few Roman-proof nations in the world, the Scots are famous for mixing religion with football, wearing a costume that the English banned, but then going off it when the Victorians

Learn Welsh while driving.

decided it was OK again, drinking whisky, eating sheep's innards and throwing huge logs at the Queen. They also hate being called Scotch, even though their national drink is called Scotch, and so are their eggs.

Scots like to travel, or rather emigrate. They rightly point out that many of them were forced to do so when the English (see *The English*) evicted them from their own land, but this does not entirely explain the Caledonian wanderlust. Scottish people can now be found all over the world, forming enormous nostalgic clan groups, singing nostalgic ballads about their homeland and doing their best not to live in Scotland any more. This is the basis of the old joke: What's the definition of a Scottish boomerang? It doesn't come back, it just sings about it.

Edinburgh is so cultural that all the Scottish people have left, renting their flats to tourists, and the streets are occupied only by English people who work for television companies

A holiday in Scotland consists largely of spectacular scenery, visiting distilleries, and lots of Scottish people in kilts and tartans selling you wee dirks and drappies and drams and so on while telling you that Scotland is nothing like this. Try to avoid saying, 'Oh, I must have been thinking of Latvia.'

Scotland is also famous for its tradition of Edinburgh and Glasgow not getting on. This is because they are very different. Glasgow is a big tough sort of place where people get into fights on a Saturday night, except they don't any more because Glasgow is a modern, thrusting city, which was European City of Culture, and is full of museums and galleries. Meanwhile, Edinburgh, which traditionally was always a city of culture, and is also full of museums and galleries, is now more famous as the home of the Edinburgh Festival. This used to be a delightful event where nice young things were shown black-and-white films about men in kilts and tartans and sporrans getting drunk in a whimsical fashion, but somehow it has expanded out through the arts, via theatre and cinema and alternative comedy into a place where thousands of foreigners turn up every year to get drunk and watch mime artists.

Underneath his kilt, this man is wearing a little thong.

At the height of the Festival, Edinburgh is so cultural that all the Scottish people have left, renting their flats to tourists, and the streets are occupied only by English people who work for television companies, interviewing each other and asking the sole remaining bagpiper to keep it down a bit.

You can tell Edinburgh was desperate to become trendy because it spent the 1990s trying to become famous for heroin, which is – if the movies are to be believed – Glasgow's job.

THE CORNISH

Cornwall is the only part of the Celtic nation to find itself attached to England. In fact, as the Duchy of Cornwall it appears to be the personal property of the Prince of Wales. (Perhaps he likes to collect small Celtic nations, and is one day hoping to be made Emperor of Scotland.) Its long relationship with England may explain why there are no original speakers of the Cornish language left. This is quite sad, but there is nothing to fear; the English, out of some massive sense of guilt, have started to pretend that Cornwall – or Kernow, as people with 2CVs like to call it – is a thriving Celtic nation. Once you have crossed the Tamar, the river that divides Cornwall from Devon apart from a little bit at the top where the English must have got in, you will find yourself assailed by KERNOW stickers, Cornish language classes and an enormous concrete bunker which houses a famous pasty factory.

2000 years of Cornish culture. In a lovely pastry shell.

This is all part of the great West Country tradition of organic heritage or 'letting a lot of hippies in'. From the crusties walking their dogs on strings on Glastonbury Tor to the naked people trying to get into Stonehenge, the West Country has a curious obsession with days of yore. Cornwall, with its actual Celtic heritage, is a natural magnet for this sort of thing. Then again, unless they recognize him as some sort of Antler God, one day there will be so many new Cornish people that they will rise up and throw the so-called Duke of Cornwall into the Thames.

THE ENGLISH

The English have for many years tended to see themselves as the dominant nation in the United Kingdom. This is true, but only because the English were the ones nearest to Normandy when William the Conqueror came over. Ever since then the English have always been a bit obsessive about the whole top dog thing.

Invading Wales, Scotland and Ireland was never going to be a great way to make friends in the international community, but the English clearly had a taste for invading people. Over the next 2,000 years or so, England, or a variant thereof, managed to go to war with or invade quite possibly every country in the world. Like a short bloke who fancies that everyone is looking down on him, or the weird kid at school who tells everyone his dad's a test pilot even though everyone's seen the weird kid's dad lying unconscious outside the pub, England has a bit of a chip about being the country that the Conqueror conquered. France, Germany, America, India, China, Russia, Spain, Argentina… England has had a pop at all of them.

This was not a great way to socialize, but it did have the advantage of ruling the world thrown in as a sort of bonus. Eventually they were made to give the world back, and did, quite graciously at times. But these days the English sort of mope around, half-heartedly trying to start fights in pub car parks or at foreign football matches, only without a lot of enthusiasm.

The fact is, the English are really good at fighting, and they're not allowed to do it. Other English skills – poetry, play-writing, asking Germans to rule them – have never really felt right. The English do like to claim that Shakespeare was the best and so on, but only in the hope that someone will put in a claim for Goethe, and then a fight might break out.

This is almost certainly why the English, among all the races and/or nations of the world, are such moaners. They bang on about the climate, perhaps remembering that they used to have the pick of the world's weather simply by going abroad and conquering some place where it was sunny. They moan about the telly, probably because a Scotsman invented it and another Scotsman started the BBC. And they don't like anyone from abroad.

But then, they aren't exactly Popular Land themselves. Their near neighbours, the rest of the UK, have learned to tolerate most of their habits, but they do get peeved in sporting events. This is because of a very English trick. Whenever a British team is winning, the English are all Brits to a man, but if that team does badly, suddenly they are Scottish again, or Welsh, or even Canadian.

When England alone are in a sporting contest, it is not a pretty sight. If England lose, expect your town to burn. And if they win – the smugness and the bragging will never end. Never mind that, on average, Estonia have probably won the World Cup more than England have; 1966 was *a golden year for English football* and no one is allowed to forget it. In 1,000 years, when black-and-white film has gone for ever, the BBC will still be showing that famous clip. They think it's all over? As long as there's an England, the 1966 World Cup will never be over. In fact the crowd invasion wasn't jubilant England fans, it was Scotsmen and Welshmen desperately trying to disrupt the match so as to stem the tide of boasting.

Recently, books have been printed in the USA with sad, self-pitying titles like *Why Does Nobody Like Us?* The English have known the answer to that one for a long time.

For a start, English people don't even like other English people...

THE NORTH

~

Where it's grim, they say proudly. Like it isn't grim in the Midlands, large parts of Wales, the Fens and most industrial or housing estates everywhere. These days, thanks to greenfield schemes and the conversion of dark satanic mills into bright satanic arts centres, the North is more twee than grim, more Tetley Tea Folk than Two Nations. In the good old days you'd have been clogged to death for wearing a buttonhole during Wakes Week in Climthorpedykenwear but these days you're more likely to be offered a job running a tea shop in the Industrial Memories Leisure Park.

Only a deep, irrational, burning hatred of Southerners kept old Thorpethwaite alive.

Northerners are very proud of 'speaking as they find'. This is Northernspeak for 'I am a miserable git and in love with myself.'

Northerners are very proud of 'speaking as they find'. This is Northernspeak for 'I am a miserable git and in love with myself.' They distrust the South for being 'soft', although they do not seem to apply this ruling to brass bands, which are the softest form of band in the world, with their Hovis themes and their classical lite music. (Hovis brings to mind another Northern obsession, nostalgia. They love to remember when it was all factories around here and you couldn't breathe for the soot coming off the wig works. Auntie May went down the pit at six weeks old and had nine lasses in number three shaft, and so on.)

Northerners only exceed their dislike of Southerners in, inevitably, their dislike of one another. Hence the rivalries between Mancunian and Liverpudlian, Newcastle and Sunderland, York and Lancaster, United and City, Everton and Liverpool FC, Carlisle and Durham, and so on, and so forth.

THE SOUTH

∿

They all go round in huge SUVs and puffa jackets, listening to second-rate imitations of American R'n'B, and they can't pronounce anything with a 't' in it. Southerners act like Lottery winners who forgot to learn to read. Their skills include shouting, screaming, getting out of the car and shouting, asking people what they are looking at in a loud voice, and bellowing their kids' names in supermarkets.

The working-class Southerners are just as bad, too, except they suffer from pointless pre-war Cockney notions of family, respect and leaving your front door open for the Krays to come in and murder everyone.

Arrogance is the cornerstone of the Southern attitude, because everyone has achieved their dream of living in a house with a conservatory glued onto the outside, a swimming pool full of dead insects and a dog named after a jailed boxer. Affluence is important too, and the widescreen television, so useful for watching Ceefax on, is everywhere.

Southerners are very proud of their children, many of whom go to stage school, and hope that one day little Chandelia or Vent will win a part in a soap opera, where they will play someone in a puffa jacket who can't pronounce the letter 't'.

A typical Southerner.

There is a North–South divide in this country, one so broad that it's a wonder the Romans didn't have a rethink and knock up Hadrian's Wall II, just north of Watford. Sadly, if they had, the Southerners would have stuck a conservatory on the side, and the Northerners would have had it pebble-dashed.

There is a North–South divide in this country, one so broad that it's a wonder the Romans didn't have a rethink and knock up Hadrian's Wall II, just north of Watford. Sadly, if they had, the Southerners would have stuck a conservatory on the side, and the Northerners would have had it pebble-dashed.

THE ISLE OF WIGHT

∽

There are many small islands surrounding the actual British Isles. Some of them are virtually rocks and some of them are virtually French (see *The Channel Islands*). Most of them have good reasons for being peculiar – Lundy is full of puffins, Man is full of tailless cats, the Shetlands have no trees – but none of this applies to the Isle of Wight. The place is virtually English. They speak English with a normal (for Hampshire) accent, they have buses and chip shops and rock festivals, and they can get satellite television.

Yet there cannot be a more miserable, damp, islandy-minded place on the planet. Maybe it's something to do with having to get on a ferry every time you want to buy a loaf of bread. Maybe it's the fact that those ponces in Guernsey get to call themselves LeClerc and visit Brittany for lunch. Either way, the Isle of Wight is the last resting place of the closed-at-3, seaside-landlady, chips-are-off mentality. Visitors to these shores are advised to go somewhere less depressing instead, like Dungeness or Stockwell.

The Gates of Hell. Closed Wednesday afternoons and Sundays.

THE ISLE OF MAN

∾

What the hell did they do to the cats? And if the cats are freaks, what must the people be like? Why have they got their own Parliament? What do they do in there all day? What's that motorbike race for?

It is forever 1953 on the Isle of Man, the place where everyone has been taken to the European Court of Human Rights twice for using the knout on toddlers. Our very own Deep South.

THE CHANNEL ISLANDS

∾

They're not part of the United Kingdom, you know. Oh no, they were leased to us by the Duke of Something in thirteen oh Good Lord is that the time. They could just run off at any time and be part of, say, the Ukraine. The Channel Islands – Jersey, Guernsey, Alderney, Sark and Mopsy – have been involved with Britain for a long time but still refuse to, as it were, take their dress off. True, they gave us all the chance to see proper British-type policemen giving directions to German soldiers during the war, and true, they prefer residents who are stinking rich fat pigs in top hats smoking cigars to anyone else, but they have decided to be British, sort of, rather than French.

So why don't they drop all the St This and Mont That nonsense and assimilate properly? Let's have regular airlifts of Burberry into Jersey. Open a Mister Pizza in Sark. Get Sky to do a series called *Guernsey Uncovered*, where large drunk women show their bottoms to people with French names.

LONDON

∾

Not to be confused with London, the holiday destination (see *A London Weekend*), London, the home of Londoners, is the most evil place in the world. This is because it combines not one, but three, horrible tribes of roving freaks.

The most notable of these are tourists. There are few places where even a tourist can feel superior to someone, and London is one of them. The tourist season begins at midnight on 31 December every year and ends a nanosecond before that time and date a year later. Tourists are everywhere. They say that you're never more than 4 feet from a rat in London. Well, move over, you and the rat, there's ten tourists who want to share your space.

Ever since the Romans came and decided that Londinium had a better ring to it than Lug, or whatever, people have been trampling

They say that you're never more than 4 feet from a rat in London. Well, move over, you and the rat, there's ten tourists who want to share your space.

through London, gawping at statues, paying too much for food, and wondering what's so great about a big damp lot of hills full of whingeing gits. The Great Fire of London didn't put anybody off; they just stuck up a statue to commemorate it, and rebuilt St Paul's, and bingo, two more tourist attractions.

'When a man is tired of London,' Dr Johnson should have written, 'he must just have got off the train. Or maybe he was mugged, or paid £3.75 for a coke, which is the same thing. Or he probably got stuck behind twenty sodding Italian tourists with bastard sodding backpacks, the gits.' London is a tourist city made horrible by tourists. Like the pigeons they don't know they're not supposed to feed, tourists hop feebly around the city, making a mess and emitting stupid cooing noises.

Worse than tourists, perhaps, are the original locals. These are known as Cockneys, although, as any cab driver will kindly take the time to tell you, a true Cockney has to be born within the sound of Bow Bells, or a tourist unzipping his money belt. Ever since Dickens immortalized the Artful Murderer and all those charming Victorian orphan lads, the world has had a sentimental view of the Cockney; and thanks to Dick Van Dyke and his curious half-strangled Rhodesian chimney sweep, the process continues.

Cockneys are the ur-Londoners. They eat jellied eels and dead sea insects. Their beer is served warm and their lager cold. They support about ten interchangeable football teams, one of whose chants is the rather honest, 'No one likes us, we don't care.' They drive taxis, own market stalls, sell Union Jack tea towels and shout a lot. They resent the tourists, but they can make a living from them. What they really hate are the incomers, the self-styled Londoners.

Incomers are people who came to London because it's such a

In some ways, it's a shame that Britons never, never, never will be slaves.

London: a seething, filthy mass of resentment, crime and Aberdeen Steakhouses.

melting pot, it's really cosmopolitan, you can see a new play every night, and the range of restaurants, it's incredible. These people are talking out of their backsides. They never go to see any plays (unless it's *The Mousetrap*), by 'cosmopolitan' they mean you can buy the *Guardian* without the newsagent attacking you, and as for the range of restaurants, they go to the same pizza restaurant once a week and nowhere else.

Incomers like to pose as locals. They are always banging on about how they have lived here for fifteen years, it's incredible how time flies. They are the ones you will see who are eager to show off their knowledge to tourists but, when pressed, do not actually know where Bond Street is. And they claim to be part of the community, but they have measured out their lives in property price increases, and their constant need for bigger, nicer houses is driving the community into the Thames.

Between the fake locals, the original locals and the visitors, it is no wonder that London is a seething, filthy mass of resentment, crime and Aberdeen Steakhouses.

EX-PATS

∽

The British are a varied people and do not get on with each other. And yet there is one group of Britons who are united despite their ethnic or religious differences: ex-pats. United in bitterness and whining, that is.

Ex-pats all seem to be engineers or work in the oil industry. The men all have moustaches and the women all sit in the shade drinking as much as possible. They spend all their time moaning about Britain but they haven't actually been back since T Rex were in the charts. If pressed on this, they claim that they don't want to as 'the country's

Ex-pats; just overpaid, racist asylum seekers in reverse.

gone to the dogs'. Point out to them that you were just there and there was no sign of canine invasion, and they grunt, and use an expression for another race that you haven't heard since *Mind Your Language* was taken off the telly.

They don't even like the place where they are living, yet will only leave when their idle fleshy backsides are kicked out during a popular uprising. This will take some time to sink in, as they have never even bothered to learn the language.

Ex-pats long for a world that never existed, and remember one that hasn't existed for many years. They still believe that all the ethnic minorities in Britain work in curry houses, that beer is one and six a pint and you can still get Double Diamond. They are like Japanese soldiers lost in the jungle, refusing to believe that the war is over.

The worst thing is that for some reason these red-faced pillocks are allowed a postal vote in British elections. Fortunately, most of them still think it's 1974 and vote for Mr Heath, so all their ballot papers are spoiled.

NOW WHAT?

THE WORLD'S MOST POPULAR
TOURIST ATTRACTIONS

~

The Eiffel Tower

Looks like the Blackpool Tower, but is much gaudier at night. Also has no nice ballroom underneath.

The Leaning Tower of Pisa

1   Oh look. Someone is pretending to hold the Tower up! Ha bloody ha. Hope it falls on them.

Later, a real building fell on this man and crushed him.

2   Only Italy could boast about inept examples of
     construction work.

The Sydney Opera House

Opera houses are meant to be big, imposing, fake classical jobs, to symbolize the joyless bellowing that goes on inside. Not like a selection of Mr Kipling's cakes gone AWOL.

The Golden Gate Bridge

Proof that the city of San Francisco is a bit short of great landmarks. 'We haven't got any landmarks!' 'Oh. Well… there's the bridge.' Not inspired.

The Pyramids

Hey! Come and see where millions of slaves were killed so some chinless hermaphrodite with his insides taken out could be dug up 10,000 years later and have a picture of his coffin put on the side of a pencil case.

The Sphinx

It hasn't got a nose.

Buckingham Palace

That's not a palace. It's a Bulgarian government building. And while we're at it – all that nonsense with the flag and is she in or out? Why not have a flag for when she's watching telly, one for when she's giving the grandson a bollocking, or one for when she's opening a new Waitrose?

Madame Tussaud's

Five hours queuing up to look at some wax that

The Sphinx. Not much cop at riddles.

Outside Madame Tussauds, thousands of people queue like static, motionless dummies, before finally getting inside to look at some more static, motionless dummies.

slightly resembles Britney Spears. The original Madame Tussaud would be delighted that her slightly creepy carnival sideshow is still going 200 years later. Everyone else just wants to sit down near some vodka.

The Dome

Pull it down! Pull it down! Or use it to store other useless failed Government ideas. A permanent exhibition of state errors. Might work.

The Parthenon

It's falling to bits. Why can't they put it in the British Museum for safe-keeping like they did with the Elgin Marbles?

Venice

You can't buy a pizza without someone droning on about Venice being in peril from flooding, or not flooding, or excess tourism, or whatever. Maybe it's time to drain the canals and pave them over.

Ten pence on your pizza for this?

That would at least stop the bastards charging 5,000 euros just to go up and down a smelly bit of water in a homosexual canoe.

HOTELS

A necessary evil. From tiny beachside hostel to enormous Germanic palace, hotels are designed with two contradictory aims in mind: to make people want to stay in them, and to get people in and out as quickly as possible. The result feels a lot like a visit to an elderly couple who say they like visitors but don't really mean it.

You are welcomed with smiles and tiny chocolates, your linen is fresh and your shower products are many. Then the day you are leaving, the phone rings to remind you to get out, cleaners start banging on the door, and you are all but thrown out of the door.

HOW NOT TO WRITE A POSTCARD

Next time someone sends you a third-rate, scrawled, lazy holiday postcard that they dashed off in between getting stuck into the raki, cut this out and send it to them.

Dear Sir or Halfwit

Thank you for your useless postcard. Next time you can afford a holiday and feel like showing off about it:

a   Try finding a vaguely recognizable image of your holiday destination. A blob of greenery or a statue's leg could be from anywhere. This will also avoid you having to look stupid and shake your fool head when someone says, `Wow! Is that where you stayed?'

b   Get off your backside and go outside the hotel and buy a postcard that is actually from where you are staying. That photo of a sexually aroused Greek god or two loveable spaniels has been recaptioned in every resort from Abergavenny to Zagreb. Look around you. Do you see any Greek gods or spaniels? No? <u>Then what is this postcard for?</u>

c   Try and write something vaguely interesting. Writing `It is hot,' will bore the eyes off me. `I am having a gender crisis,' will not.

d   Remember to take an address book with you, unless you actually collect postcards with stamps and people's names on, and no actual address. I can tell if you forgot my address because the card arrives two years after you left, with the address written on it in green ink and a British stamp on it. It's no good sending a card after you've got home. Receiving such a postcard does not say, `We were thinking of you on holiday,' it says, `We forgot about you on holiday.'

e   Get me liquor next time, you tight sod.

BUMBAGS

∾

W hat's *that*? You look like this morning you got up and said, 'No, mother. Today I shall dress myself.' Take it off.

Either that or you wish to provide a sort of mobile cashpoint service for thieves. 'I wanted to protect my wallet and phone, so I attached them to the outside of my clothes and provided a zip for easy stranger access.' You muppet.

HOLIDAY SNAPS

∾

T here are few things more boring than other people's holiday snaps (other people's holiday movies come to mind). This is partly because being a captive audience for anything less exciting than a fight to the death between a bear and a dragon is very annoying. There's also the knowledge that the whole thing will take ages, will not involve strong liquor, and will involve someone with a droning voice using it to drone.

But, worst of all, we are not talking great photography here. This is not like being sat down by Helmut Newton or David Bailey to admire their new work. This is the work of some oaf with a cheap camera, or an expensive one he cannot use properly. 'Untutored' is not the word. 'Pointing at things and going click' is.

Here, for the oaf's benefit, is a brief guide to making holiday snaps slightly less unendurable.

1. Originality

What's in this photo? Well, there's the Parthenon, looking very much like the Parthenon, only bigger and grubbier. And there's you, looking very much like you, only smaller and redder. And that's it. Nothing much else going on. You, and the Parthenon. From five different angles. Wow. If we had never seen a picture of the Parthenon before we might be going, 'Oh my God! What is that building?' But we have. And we've seen the Eiffel Tower, the

Leaning Tower of Pisa, the Empire State Building and all the other big things you have taken pictures of. And we've seen you. The pairing is not a thrilling one.

2. Composition

If we're going to have to sit through an hour of you and/or your wife standing in front of things, at least take a few seconds to think about the picture. Maybe you could include all of your wife's head in the shot. Maybe the Eiffel Tower ought not to be coming out of the top of her head. Perhaps you could have waited until the dustcart had left the Piazza San Marco. Little things like that.

The sign is there to remind him where he took this picture of sod all and nothing.

3. Repetition

Only an international art thief needs pictures of the Louvre taken from fourteen different positions. Either take fewer photos, or steal the Mona Lisa.

4. Context

To you, your hotel room may be a place whose image you want to keep for ever. To us it's a hotel room.

5. Presentation

Oh God, not the slide projector. Why not properly go for it and hire the London Planetarium to project your dull snaps into the mighty star-studded night?

6. Anecdote fuel

A photograph can be a jumping-off point for a great story. It rarely bloody is, though. Any story beginning, 'This is a couple we met…' is never going to be interesting to anyone but you and the other couple. In a fair world, the sight of two strangers in someone else's holiday snaps ought to be reason enough for your audience to knock you to the ground.

7. Baffling pictures

The ones where you say, 'I have no idea who/what/where this is.' If you don't know, you great creeping gas wimple, what possible interest can anyone else have? It's not 'Guess the Mystery Object', is it? Sadly.

8. Your children

They are not doing anything interesting in the picture. Really.

9. Your pets

See 8.

10. You

See 8 and 9.

HOLIDAY FRIENDSHIPS

∾

Golden rule: If you hear a British accent on holiday, run away. Otherwise you will end up 'befriending' some terrifying couple who have nothing in common with you apart from the same passport. If these people were your neighbours at home, you would move, so why talk to them now?

Holiday romance; Guido has no job. Then again, Alan is a post-operative transsexual.

There is no movie called Stanley Valentine, where Liverpool bloke Stanley goes to Knossos and becomes romantically involved with a beautiful barmaid whose dream is to see the Wirral.

HOLIDAY ROMANCES

It is rare that romance with a Greek waiter or Spanish barman will blossom into something everlasting. And even in fiction this sort of thing is confined to the older ladies. Any waiters or barmen reading should bear in mind that they are likely to be forgotten by young Theresa upon her return to Reading, where the giddy whirl of study and dancing means that once more she will fall in love with somebody unsuitable who works in Caffe Nero but really wants to be a bass player.

Men should note that the whole 'Shirley Valentine' syndrome works, as the name suggests, only when the protagonist is female. There is no movie called Stanley Valentine, where Liverpool bloke Stanley goes to Knossos and becomes romantically involved with a beautiful barmaid whose dream is to see the Wirral. Or if there is, the beautiful hostess will arrive in England and cop off with Stan's brother Terry, and Stan will never be able to show his face in the pub again.

SWIMMING COSTUMES

Of all the things that you can forget to bring on holiday, the swimming costume is the most annoying. You forget it every time, and have to buy a new one. This is common to most holiday-related items, but with swimwear the buggers are just expensive enough to annoy the hell out of you. And they don't even make trunks, they make tiny bags for your testicles that you can't swim in for fear of making yourself into an aqua-soprano.

THE HOTEL SAFE

Takes five hours to work out how to use it, and then the moment you have finally solved it, and you can actually get your wallet out again, it moves and you realize it has not been attached to the wall.

HAVING A DRINK

Fraught. Every country in the world has not only weird rules about opening hours, but really weird rules about how much your drinks cost depending on where you are sitting. Take an uncomfortable stool at the bar, and you will pay 10 euros for your glass of froth. Sit at the little table near the back and your froth will cost you 20 euros. Relax on the terrace outside and the sky's the limit. It is not clear if this tariff has any logical limits; for example, will it cost you 60 euros to take your drink for a walk? And is it only 5 euros if you have your drink while standing behind the bar?

Get maximum enjoyment from this idiot rule by sitting in all the seats in the bar and making the waiter pick the bones out of that one.

Trunks – £5.99. Trouser squirrel – model's own.

TOURIST MENUS

∽

You look in through the window of the restaurant, which is filled with roasted ducks and carafes of red wine. Happy, red-faced locals are enjoying banquets of Romanesque opulence. They quaff and chew and laugh and, at the end, leave about four bob to pay the bill. You go in. You are shown a table so near to the toilets that you can wash your hands without getting up. You are about to ask for a drink when a waiter shoves a huge piece of laminated cardboard in your hand. It has none of the food the locals just ate on it. It is the tourist menu, and it is awful. All the food on it is available in cheap cafés in the Midlands, only at a quarter of the price. You stand up and stun the waiter with the water jug, then grab a carafe and a roast duck from the window and run for it.

TIPPING IN HOTELS

∽

Americans don't tip hotel staff. This is probably because they have tipped everyone else, from the cab driver to the barman, and are now broke. That said, hotel tipping is a moot area. Do you leave a decent tip for the poor cleaning woman, or do you just dump all your weird local brown money onto the dresser? Warning: Only ever tip after you have packed and are on your way downstairs, unless you wish to come back from breakfast and find your passport floating in the toilet bowl.

SAND

∽

The true devil's dandruff. People speak of the Three S's – sun, sea and sand – as though the three were equally good. The sun is bountiful (but see *Suntan*), the sea is nice to swim in and the sand is… well, the sand is little bits of earth that have been ground up specially over millions of years to annoy you. Sand gets everywhere –

in your hair, under your nails, in your navel, in your eyes, in your drink, in your sandwiches, in the binding of your holiday paperback, in your Walkman and in your camera. Sand is vile. The first person to invent a way of making sand less sandy will almost certainly receive the Nobel Prize.

TOILETS

There's something about toilets abroad which suggests that, like the Queen, foreigners do not ever have to relieve themselves. If they did, they'd have progressed beyond the most basic points of loo construction. Most of them have an attitude towards lavatory design which would shock a pig. A very big, lazy pig that likes lying down in its own dinner. It is possible to visit countries, true, where the humblest peasant hut conceals a lav of such grandeur as to make the visitor gasp (see 1 below). But it is more likely that, in a land where the palaces are opulent and guilded, the khazis will be more like some sort of troll's well (see 6 below).

Here, to aid the weary traveller, is an unofficial top six of what Americans euphemistically call 'bathrooms'.

1   *Japan.* With their powerful fondness for personal hygiene, it is not surprising that the Japanese have the best toilets in the world. Using a combination of modern technology, rigorous hygiene and an urge towards the pristine that would make a vacuum seem cluttered and filthy, Japanese toilets do everything but actually go for you. One day, they will.

2   *Germany.* Another land renowned for a certain fussiness in matters of personal cleanliness. Germans achieved a new reputation for hygiene strangeness among foreign exchange students (see *Exchange visits*) when many visiting British teenagers discovered that German toilets are built the wrong way round. This is so... no, some things are better left unsaid.

3   *The UK.* We invented them, probably. We certainly take a pride

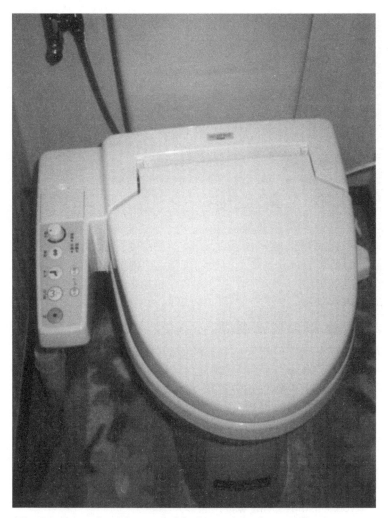

The Japanese toilet. They probably do eat their dinner off it.

in them. The Victorian public toilet is, legendarily, a place where an honest working man can take his ease in comfort, amid surroundings which would shame a continental mansion. And even now the introduction of the street pay toilet is a

'Bienvenue!'

thoughtful device, enabling tourists to get stuck and panic in the very heart of an alien city.

4   *America.* Their lavs are not bad, but are marked down owing to the unusual American predilection for beige. Bathroom fittings are not beige, they are white. American toilets look like they were all designed in the 1970s for use by Starsky and Hutch. And the urinals have switches on so you can flush them yourself, thus saving water but wasting time and electricity.

5   *Most of the rest of the world.* The missing seat, the string flush, the busted door… many parts of the world suffer terribly from poor sanitary facilities. Civil war, famine and the collapse of the Berlin Wall are to blame, but are no excuse, really.

6   *France.* Some – the French, probably – may protest that France has much better loos than the Gabon, or Turkestan, or Nagorno-

Karabakh. Others may point at, for instance, war zones where there are often no toilet facilities. They are missing the point. France is a bastion of civilization. They have made massive contributions to art, philosophy, music, painting, theatre and dance music. And yet, khazi-wise, they still exhibit a fondness for a hole in the ground. There is no excuse for this, even from the country that invented the *pissoir*.

NUDISM

∾

Arrgh! Nudist beaches, camps and 'colonies' are havens of sex, if you are Sid James. Otherwise they are very frightening places where self-satisfied vegans and people who buy books about conspiracies like to lie and be smug. Walk near one wearing any clothing at all, and the nudists go mental. You're wearing clothes! You pervert!

As God intended us to be. Only fat, wrinkly and naked.

It wouldn't be so bad if the bastards had the decency to maybe go to the gym or eat fewer vegan pasties. There is nothing more guaranteed to put you off sex than a walk across a crowded nudist beach. The place looks like a refuge for balding orang-utans.

And they shave themselves! All over! Argh! Uk!

SUNTAN

Once upon a time, having tanned skin was a sign of poverty. Peasants toiled in the sun, went brown, and were clearly marked as poor. The gentry stayed indoors and had skin like veal. Then tanning became popular. It was a sign that you were well travelled and sophisticated and could afford to spend a month lying on a deck somewhere soaking up rays.

Nowadays it's all changed again, what with skin cancer and global warming, and a tan means either that you can't afford proper sun cream (see *Sun cream*) or that you spend all your spare time in a tanning booth, you common person, you.

SUN CREAM

Like injections (see *Jabs*), sun cream is a holiday evil. When you are relaxing by the pool you want to feel nice. You want to relax. You do not want to get up and, just before strolling outside, be told by a relative or spouse to 'put some cream on, it's roasting outside'. You then spend twenty minutes covering yourself in some unpleasant smelly white paste, which never stops being sticky, gets in your eyes and generally makes you feel like you have been ineptly basted.

Now you can go outside. After a while the sun cream starts to fizzle on your skin, so you go for a swim. This cools you down, but also enables millions of grains of sand (see *Sand*) to become stuck to your skin. Now you have to shower to get it all off, and this means that if you go out again, which you will, because it isn't even lunchtime yet, you will have to – yes – put on more bloody sun cream.

And there's the quality dilemma. The cheap stuff is vile and sticky and comes off as soon as you get into the pool, and the expensive stuff is even stickier, and never comes off, ever. You have to scrape it off you with a bread knife.

SOUVENIRS 1

You wouldn't buy a bear dressed as a Swiss Guard at home, so why buy one on holiday? What possible reason could you have for owning a model Jamaican made from whelks? And what is that T-shirt with a map of Gabon for? The answer is, sadly, 'It's a souvenir.'

'Where did you buy this again?'

The word 'souvenir' comes from the French for 'remember', suggesting that your holiday was so dull that you would forget all about it if you hadn't bought a tea-towel or a mug with the name of the resort printed on it.

Souvenirs are a unique form of junk. They can be surreal – a fridge magnet shaped like the Arc de Triomphe, say, or a thermometer shaped like the Manneken Pis. They may have some vague local relevance, like a leather camel (with its own crew of fleas) or an enormous sombrero. And they may scream ATTENTION! LOOK AT ME! in the form of a T-shirt with a horrible slogan (*My Folks Went to Ho Chi Minh City and All They Got Me Was This Lousy T-Shirt, Good Girls Go to Heaven Bad Girls Go to Leamington Spa*).

Whatever form they take, souvenirs are best abandoned, along with the half-empty sun cream bottle, unfinished Dean Koontz novel and postcards whose addressees' addresses you have lost, at the airport.

SOUVENIRS 2 – BUMPER STICKERS
～

Now people know where you've been. Why not just glue your diary to the bumper of your car?

All holiday-bought drink is undrinkable. It is generally a fluorescent shade of something internal

LOCAL ALCOHOL
～

One of the great mysteries of life is this; the world is full of great booze. Many, many countries produce highly potable wines, sherries, beers, ports, brandies and so forth. So how come nobody ever comes back from holiday with any of them?

All holiday-bought drink is undrinkable. It is generally a fluorescent shade of something internal, contains enough alcohol to sterilize a football stadium, and tastes like an old wig left in a sewer for the whole of the 1960s.

This is perhaps why the future home of such booze is either the very back of the drinks cabinet or under the sink. Or, more likely, your house, in the form of 'a present we got you abroad. It's all right when you get used to it.'

It isn't.

LOCAL PRODUCE

Don't be upset when the customs man (see *Customs and excise officers*) confiscates your pungent salami and fines you. He is doing us all a favour.

HOLIDAY INSURANCE SCAMS

It's hard to pull one of these off, unless you can persuade granny and the kids to push the hired Seat off a cliff in the hope of claiming some extra euros in compensation for the loss of a second-hand video camera and some old flippers. The most popular scam is, apparently, going to France on a ski holiday and claiming on the last day that your brand new skis have been nicked. Over 3,000 skis are reported stolen every year, it seems, and 15 per cent of claims are fraudulent. The British are the worst offenders – at claiming, that is, not stealing – but the Germans, Italians and Dutch are close behind.

What this statistic actually reveals: a) We get the blame while all around us are at it as well. b) The Dutch? Where do they get skis from? c) If 15 per cent of ski thefts are fraudulent, then 85 per cent aren't. In short, don't go to France or a Dutchman will nick your skis.

Abroad, where the toilet attendants dress like field marshals

'OFFICIALS'

Somewhere in the world, in more than the one country, there must be a Ministry of Backhanders. How else to explain the ruthless efficiency with which a bunch of dressed-up criminals and bone-idle fake bureaucrats manage to take money off people for doing naff all? Maybe their stupid clothing has special pockets for stuffing bribes into. Perhaps their sinister black gloves are ideal for concealing the filthy marks made by their cheap local money. Either way, if you are an emergent nation, or just want to join the EU, it might be a good idea to ease off on the bribery thing, else everyone thinks you are a bunch of not-quite-civilized gangsters in comedy trousers.

FOREIGN POLICEMEN

It's a long-established belief that the British police are the best in the world. With their stout conical hats, their stubby truncheons

Yes, we are all foreign policemen. And yes, it is legal in all our countries.

and their friendly short-sleeved summer uniforms, they are a model law enforcement agency. Cross the channel, however, and it is all completely different.

For a kick-off, there's the guns. Our chaps occasionally have weapons issued to them – and always like to make sure this won't be a regular occurrence by accidentally shooting innocent members of the public. But abroad they've all got guns. Railway police, traffic police, ceremonial police – armed to the foreign teeth.

And more disturbingly, they're all dressed like General Sir Hillary Hot Pot. A small child watching some *carabinieri* or *gendarmes* on parade might be forgiven for thinking that a lot of tin soldiers have come to life. One expects them to drill to the 'March of the Sugar Plum Fairy', rather than gas and club several angry fishermen.

The golden rule for travellers abroad is: Beware – the fussiness of the uniform is in inverse proportion to the unarmedness of the fuzz. Hence the bloke with half an Apache headdress and more gold braid than a wedding-dress shop for admirals is a half-trained, fully Uzi-ed gun nutter. However, a man dressed quite normally, say with just the one peacock feather in his kepi, is harmless, because he is a stationmaster.

CUSTOMS AND EXCISE OFFICERS

M iserable sods, the lot of them. The fact that in their spare time they also appear to do your VAT is not a coincidence. They have two obsessions: catching you out, and nicking you. When not searching through the luggage of someone who must be a drug dealer because they're wearing a turban, they are searching through the luggage of someone who must be a terrorist because they bought too much duty free. Their dream is to get you in the back room and strip search you. Some people join special societies to do that sort of thing; these people get paid to do it.

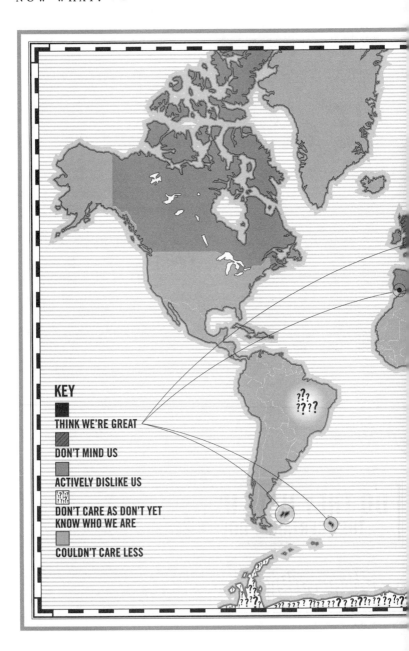

KEY

THINK WE'RE GREAT

DON'T MIND US

ACTIVELY DISLIKE US

DON'T CARE AS DON'T YET
KNOW WHO WE ARE

COULDN'T CARE LESS

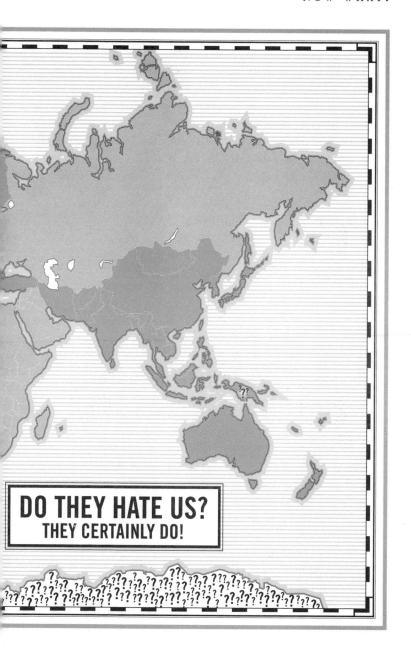

DO THEY HATE US?
THEY CERTAINLY DO!

LANGUAGE

∽

There is, as we all know, only one way to talk to people abroad – in English, only more loudly. This almost always works, as foreigners only respect you if you bellow at them.

Should you, by some nightmarish fluke, find yourself with some foreigners who don't speak English, there is a simple Plan B – talk to them in English, only more loudly, and put the letter 'O' at the end of each noun. (In Germany, preface each word with 'Der' instead). If you wish to be formal, you may address the other person by what might possibly be their name.

Here are a few examples:

- 'Buongiorno. We have uno reservationo, for four-o people-o.'
- 'Buenas dias. What time-o does the bar open-o?'
- 'Oi Fritz! Get off der sunbed!'

(But not: 'Hey Manuel! Bring us some more vino-o!' 'Vino' is a word known to all foreigners, and thus does not need the second 'O'.)

You will instantly be admired for your willingness to tackle the local lingo. Generally, however, English will suffice. And even in the above circumstance there are certain English words which are universally understood:

- Beer
- Chips
- Fish and chips
- Burger and chips
- Vino
- Pizza
- How much?
- You bastards!
- Two World Wars, one World Cup!
- Oi copper!
- Get off me!

- I am a British citizen!
- Ing-er-land!
- Let me out of here!
- I demand to speak to the British Ambassador!

and so forth.

If, by some terrible fluke, you find that you are surrounded by foreign numptyheads who do not speak – or, more likely, are pretending not to speak – any English, you may wish to commit a few foreign expressions to memory. The following are all the words and phrases that any British traveller abroad will need to make their dissatisfaction felt anywhere in the world.

I think you have poisoned me.

Japanese: Doku wo nomasetana!

German: Ich glaube, Sie haben mich vergiftet.

Spanish: Creo que me ha envenenado.

Russian: Mnye kazhetsa shto vy menya otravili.

Are you sure this qualifies as entertainment?

Thai: ngan nhee ngan ban-tueng jring rue bplau?

German: Sind Sie sicher, dass man das als Unterhaltung bezeichnen kann?

Spanish: ¿Está seguro de que esto se puede calificar de diversión?

Italian: Ma vi sembra che questo si possa chiamare divertimento?

Does the disco go on till 3 a.m. every morning?

French: Est-ce que les soirées disco durent jusqu'à trois heures tous les matins?

Greek: I diskotek litourgi kathe nihta os tis tris ta ximeromata?

Spanish: ¿Continúa la discoteca hasta las tres cada mañana?

Italian: La discoteca è aperta fino alle tre di ogni mattina?

Excuse me, our waiter seems to have been abducted.

French: Pardon, il semblerait que notre serveur a été enlevé.

Greek: Me syghorite, fenete pos apigagan to gkarsoni mas.

Spanish: Perdone, parece que han secuestrado a nuestro camarero.

Italian: Scusi, a quanto pare il nostro cameriere è stato rapito.

We asked for the bill, not the cost of a new house.

French: Nous avons demandé l'addition, pas le coût d'une maison neuve.

German: Wir hatten um die Rechnung gebeten, nicht um den Kostenvoranschlag für ein neues Haus.

Spanish: Pedimos la cuenta, no el precio de una casa nueva.

Italian: Volevamo il conto, non il costo di una nuova casa.

Does it normally rain so much in the dry season?

Swahili: Je, kwa kawaida, m-vua hu-nye-sha sana katika m-simu wa joto?

Indonesian: Apakah biasanya sering hujan dalam musim kemarau?

Spanish: ¿Suele llover tanto durante la estación seca?

Thai: nha ron, fon dtok nhak yang nee bpen bpra jum rue?

Can you recommend anywhere that isn't owned by a relation or member of your family?

French: Pouvez-vous nous recommander un endroit qui ne soit pas tenu par une de vos connaissances ou un membre de votre famille?

Arabic: hal yumkinak an taqtarih makanan laysa mamloukan liwahidin min aqaribak aw 'ailatak?

Spanish: ¿Puede recomendar algún lugar que no pertenezca a un familiar o un miembro de su familia?

Hindi: Kyaa tum mujhey aisi koi jagah bataa saktey ho jo tumharey parivaar yaa kisee rishteydaar kee naa ho?

Is this a main road or have I joined a motor racing circuit?

French: Est-ce une route principale ou viendrais-je de déboucher sur un circuit de courses automobiles?

German: Ist das eine Hauptstraße oder befinde ich mich auf einer Rennstrecke?

Spanish: ¿Es ésta la carretera principal o me he metido en un circuito de automovilismo?

Italian: Questa è la strada principale o mi sono infilato in una pista per automobili?

Where is the toilet? Ha ha! No really, where is the toilet?

French: Où sont les toilettes? Ha! Ha! Non, sérieusement, où sont les toilettes?

Hindi: Toilet kahaan hai. Ha! Ha! Naheen sachmuch, toilet kahaan hai?

Japanese: Toire wa doko? Ha! Ha! Oshiete! Toire wa doko?

Italian: Dove sono i servizi? Ha ha! Non, sul serio, dove sono i servizi?

Would it be fair to assume that you are not insured?

Indonesian: Benarkah anda tidak memiliki asuransi?

Thai: mai mee bpra-gan jring rue?

Spanish: ¿Sería razonable pensar que usted no tiene seguro?

Italian: Mi sembra il caso di dire che Lei non sia assicurato?

Do you have any souvenirs that I won't throw away as soon as I get home?

French: Est-ce que vous vendez des souvenirs que je suis susceptible de ne pas jeter sitôt arrivé chez moi?

Hindi: Kyaa aapke paas koi aisi yaadgaar cheez hai jise main ghar jaakar fainkoon naheen?

Spanish: ¿Vende algún recuerdo que no yo vaya a tirar a la basura al volver a casa?

Italian: Avete dei souvenir da non buttar via, non appena ritorno a casa?

Do the lizards have priority in the bathroom?

French: Les lézards sont-ils prioritaires dans la salle de bains?

Swahili: Je, m-jusi ndi-ye ana-ye-pewa nafasi na umuhimu za-idi ndani ya bafu?

Spanish: ¿Tienen prioridad los lagartos en el cuarto de baño?

Italian: La precedenza in bagno è riservata alle lucertole?

This is the worst meal I have ever eaten. And once I fell mouth-first into a cowpat.

French: C'est le pire repas que j'ai jamais fait, et pourtant, une fois je suis tombé la tête la première dans une bouse de vache.

German: Das ist das Schlimmste, was ich jemals gegessen habe. Und dabei bin ich einmal mit dem Gesicht in einem Kuhfladen gelandet.

Spanish: Ésta es la comida más mala que he comido en mi vida. Y eso que una vez me caí de cabeza en una boñiga.

Italian: Questo è il peggior pasto ch'io abbia mai avuto. E figuratevi che una volta caddi, faccia in giù, nello sterco di una mucca.

I would have to be drunk to pay this bill, which, given the amount of water in this wine, I am not.

French: Il faudrait que je sois ivre pour payer cette addition, ce qui, compte tenu de la quantité d'eau qu'il y a dans ce vin, n'est pas le cas.

German: Um diese Rechnung zu bezahlen, müsste ich betrunken sein, was jedoch bei dem hohen Wasseranteil in diesem Wein unmöglich ist.

Spanish: Haría falta estar borracho para pagar esta cuenta, y con la cantidad de agua que lleva este vino, no lo estoy.

Italian: Dovrei essere unbriaco per pagare il conto, ma vista la quantita di acqua nel vino, ubriaco non lo sono.

Enjoy a wildlife safari in the comfort of your own loo.

Is the queue normally this long or are you trying for a world record?

French: La file d'attente est toujours aussi longue ou vous essayez d'établir un record du monde?

German: Sind die Warteschlangen immer so lang oder ist dies ein Weltrekordversuch?

Russian: U vass obychno ocheredi takiye dllnniye, Ili vy pytaeyetess poblt' mirovoi record?

Italian: La coda è normalmente cosi lunga o state stabilendo un nuovo record mondiale?

This hotel room resembles the one in the brochure in the same way that I resemble Indira Gandhi.

French: Cette chambre d'hôtel ressemble à celle de la brochure comme je ressemble à Indira Gandhi.

German: Das Hotelzimmer und das Bild im Prospekt haben die gleiche Ähnlichkeit wie ich und Indira Gandhi.

Spanish: Esta habitación se parece a la del folleto igual que yo me parezco a Indira Gandhi.

Italian: Questa stanza assomiglia a quella nell'opuscolo dell'hotel quanto io assomiglio a Indira Gandhi.

I am unable to tell the toilet from the shower.

French: Je n'arrive pas à distinguer les toilettes de la douche.

German: Ich kann die Toilette nicht von der Dusche unterscheiden.

Spanish: No puedo distinguir el váter de la ducha.

Italian: Non riesco a distinguere il gabinetto dalla doccia.

I asked you to take me to the museum, not stop in the middle of the road and buy a live chicken.

Indian: Maine aapse mujhey Museum le jaaney ke liye kahaa thaa, na ki isliye ki aap sadak ke beech mein ruk jaayen aur chicken khareedne lageen.

Arabic: laqad talabtu minka an takhuthani ila el mat haf, la an taqif fi wasat el tareeq wa tashtari dejaja hayya.

Spanish: Le pedí que me llevara al museo, no que parara en medio del camino a comprar un pollo vivo.

Swahili: Nili-kuomba unipeleka hadi chumba cha kuhi-fadhia vitu vya kale, wala siyo usimame kando ya barabara ili kumnunua kuku aliye ha-i.

If I had wanted to eat to the accompaniment of a Mariachi band, I would have hired some people who could actually play their instruments.

Spanish: Si hubiera querido cenar acompañado por un mariachi, habría pagado a uno que sepa tocar sus instrumentos.

I thought I was buying a soft drink, not the whole country.

French: Je pensais que j'achetais une boisson fraîche, pas le pays entier.

German: Ich dachte, ich hätte einen Softdrink gekauft, nicht das gesamte Land.

Spanish: Pensé que compraba un refresco, no el país entero.

Italian: Pensavo di comprare una bibita, non l'intero Paese.

If this fish is cooked, then I am the London Symphony Orchestra.

French:　　Si ce poisson est cuit, alors moi je suis l'orchestre symphonique de Londres.

Japanese: Moshi Kono sakana ga ryori sitearunara watashi wa London kokyo-gakudan.

Spanish:　Si este pescado está hecho, entonces yo soy la Orquesta Sinfónica de Londres.

Greek:　　An afto to psari ine magiremeno, tote ego ime i Symfoniki Orhistra tou Londinou.

Excuse me, this water tastes of flower wee.

French:　Pardon, cette eau a goût de pipi de fleur.

German: Entschuldigung, das Wasser schmeckt nach Blumenpisse.

Spanish: Perdóneme, este agua sabe al pipí de flores.

Italian:　Scusi, il sapore di quest'acqua è simile a quello della pipi dei fiori.

RETURNING HOME

THE GAS

~

Yes. You have left it on.

PICTURE CREDITS